"The book 'Low-Carb Sweets' kicks dieters into dessert heaven..."

Health Store News
★ ★ ★

"You can now have your cake and eat it, too. Wonderful recipes that help eliminate diabetes, obesity, heart problems..."

Artista J. Marchioni, RN
President, Artistas's Nutrition
★ ★ ★

"Sharon Allbright's book not only brings joy to the palate but feeds the mind and soul as well."

Dr. Daniel W. Layne, Ph.D.
Oriental Medicine, Yoga Master
★ ★ ★

"A delight to read. You've managed to tackle both the practical and the emotional, creating prose good for the literal and metaphorical hearts."

Catherine Coan
Author of "Aviation"
★ ★ ★

"Now, my mom lets me eat cookies. I help make them, too."

Samantha, Age 9
★ ★ ★

"Thank you for the fabulous, life-changing recipes. My body feels like a palace instead of a prison."

Cynthia in Detroit, via Email
★ ★ ★

Sharon Allbright's

LOW ♥ CARB

SWEETS

The Art of Self-Indulgence

Paisley Print House, Los Angeles, California

First Edition

{ *This book does not recommend any type of dietary plan-- that is a decision only you and your health care practitioner can make.* }

Title page art by Luis Vargas.
Back cover photo by John Stinson.
Graphics by Stephen Sweeney.

Paisley Print House
Los Angeles, California

www.LowCarbSweets.net

Printed in the United States of America.
First Printing: February 2003

In memory of my beloved son

Bart Michael Lewis

I want to thank the many people who helped with the creation of this book.

Most of all, my husband, Stephen Sweeney, whose computer expertise played a major part in making this dream a reality.

Luis Vargas deserves huge kudos for his exquisite artwork that lifts this publication to a higher aesthetic level.

Editor, Catherine Coan, who stepped in (at the last minute) with her words of encouragement and friendship.

John Stinson, my favorite photographer, who has always been there.

"My help cometh from the Lord, which made heaven and earth."

Psalm 121.2

Notes from the author:

This isn't going to be a "She lives by the ocean with her husband and dog" introduction-- though I do.

The important information is that I have had a life-long battle with a sweet tooth and finally won. By that, I don't mean to imply that I have feasted on cream puffs and in two months whittled down from a "size 20" to a "size 2"-- I didn't.

But, I have feasted on the low-carb desserts of my dreams and trimmed down from a size 18 to 14 in about a year. I also know that if I continue exercising and staying with a low-carb plan, I will reach my goal.

I'm not saying that I never have bouts of "food crazies"-- I do. But the bouts are emotional-- not unquenchable sugar cravings. And if I do go over board on low-carb sweets, I'm not faced with guilt or a sugar hangover.

By learning to handle the emotional side of eating and sharing my struggles and successes laid the foundation for the "Art of Self Indulgence" section of this book.

Making indulgence a healthy principle has brought strong support from countless others who struggle with the problem of self-denial.

Many of us have found this new "low-carb life style" to be easy, non-deprivational and in truth-- phenomenal.

This sweet plan is a way of having it all:
- A variety of goodies, from brownies to cream puffs.
- Plenty of protein.
- Loads of fabulous fiber.

The main thing this plan eliminates is guilt. Learning to allow ourselves this newfound pleasure might take a little time. Got the time? Welcome aboard.

Sharon Allbright

Contents

Recipes   57

Cookies • *Fabulous Fudgies* • *The Easy Almond Biscotti* • *Chocolate Walnut Biscotti* • *Poppy Seed Butter Cookies* • *Chocolate Angel Clouds* • *Coconut Chip Cookies* • *Chunky Chocolate Brownies* • *Ginger Snappies* • *Chocolate Chip Bars* • *Sweet Heart Cookies* • *Orange-Frosted Fudge Brownies* •

Recipes Continued,..

A Celebration

Low-carb advocates are celebrating the release of Sharon Allbright's new book, "Low-Carb Sweets and The Art of Self-Indulgence."

Sumptuous recipes like Macadamia Fudge, Fresh Strawberry Pie and Chocolate Crème Brulee are but a few of the dozens of recipes in this groundbreaking publication.

The best news is that each treat contains less than 5 grams of carbs. There is even a "Zero Carb Waffle" for those suffering from breakfast boredom.

This project is a long labor of love for the author, who confesses, "I love sweets-- but eating old fashioned flour and sugar-filled desserts caused uncontrollable binges, blood sugar plunges and, of course, weight gain."

For the health conscious, this book has added appeal because of the nutritious ingredients used to create these low-carb goodies. Allbright left no grain unturned or sweetener untouched to find just the right combinations for this treasure trove of slimming indulgences.

Unlike many commercial products, these desserts are not loaded with artificial additives but contain high quality protein, natural sweeteners, healthy oils and heaps of fiber.

Another important feature of this book is that it's written for the novice, as well as the experienced cook. Many of the recipes are both fast and easy to prepare.

In fact, "Chocolate Almond Clusters" can be put together in five minutes and contain only 2.5 grams of carbs each.

The second segment of this unique book is "The Art of Self Indulgence." Information for this section came to light through the author's surprising struggle with this "sweeter way of slimming." After talking to dozens of others, she found out she wasn't alone.

"It turns out that years of dieting had made us feel unworthy of eating foods we actually liked. Self-deprivation had become a way of life," says Allbright.

The touching stories of breaking barriers of self-denial make this a cookbook with a heart.

In The Beginning

This book began with my personal struggle to turn low-carb eating into a lifestyle of pleasure.

I wanted to satisfy my cravings for delicious desserts and sumptuous sweets but I also wanted these treats to be healthy, slimming and to provide heaps of fiber. (Lack of bulk can be a huge issue without grains and other fibrous foods.)

Every time I perfected a new sweet recipe, people would taste the results-- and inevitably remark, "You should write a book."

With a background in newspaper and magazine journalism-- and a lifelong struggle with foods, I decided that maybe this could be a worthwhile venture.

I first adopted the high-protein/low-carb eating plan several years ago. Within a year, I whittled down from a generous "size 18" to a svelte "size 10."

I maintained the weight loss for several years but suffered from dessert deprivation and food boredom.

Eventually that deprivation and all the "high-carb/low-fat propaganda" hooked me in. So, I bit the organic bullet, went on a high-carb regime and ended up (once again) overweight and addicted to carbohydrates.

I made up my mind that I was going back to the low-carb plan, but this time I would somehow tweak it to include my favorite, formerly forbidden foods.

There were two main areas in the low-carb life style that troubled me. The first was breakfast. I could never face a plate of eggs first thing in the morning. The other was finding fast-food snacks. When I was working (and I do a lot of freeway travel) I would end up buying a bag of nuts as a meal substitute because I couldn't stop for a salad or other healthy meal.

Finding ways to solve those problems was a joy in itself, but to actually come up with desserts of my dreams put me over the top of the happiness scale.

I not only discovered ways to make old favorites like brownies and biscotti-- but also created new delights like Chocolate Crème Brulee... Yum!

A huge bonus is that I feel healthier because of the generous amounts of fiber and protein that are incorporated into these satisfying weets.

The next chapter elaborates on the trials and triumphs of finding the perfect ingredients for these rare goodies.

Another story also emerged in the lengthy process of writing this book.

As it turns out, there is a lot more to sweets than combining ingredients.

What emerged from the mix was a huge amount of guilt connected to eating these goodies-- even while I was slimming down to the body of my dreams.

This enigma wasn't mine alone. While researching this project, I talked to countless others who also confronted gigantic obstacles of self-denial. We discovered that most of us also had problems allowing ourselves pleasure in other areas of our lives. It was somehow wired into our psyche that some of us are not entitled to eat things we enjoy-- much less allow ourselves to have the lives we dream of.

Self-denial had become a way of life.

It became obvious that I must learn to graciously accept the privilege of this new sweet life while learning to identify and destroy the guilt and ego traps along the way.

Learning self-indulgence became a lengthy course. It takes time to gain the upper hand on self-denial. But for the victor comes sweet surrender-- not to mention a slimmer body.

On the Low-Carb Trail
(In Search of Dessert Nirvana)

The first step in winning the battle against high-carb sweet cravings was finding a way to replace flour and sugar.

I have a journalistic background and through the years have developed a real interest in health and nutrition. I have even written a column in a health magazine. Yet as I looked through countless publications for clues, I found that editors totally ignored the subject of sweets in a low-carbohydrate diet. In fact, one even called it an oxymoron.

I was on my own.

But, I was on a mission and (little by little) started to discover the ingredients that would finally help me crack the case of providing "a banquet of sweets on a low-carb budget."

I wanted something that would smell like bread baking, have a scrumptious texture and the perfect sweetenes to turn my morning coffee into a drink for royalty.

Replacing flour was my first challenge. Some diet books suggest using soy flour for bulk, but I find the results of recipes with soy flour neither tasty nor satisfying.

I left no powder or grain unturned. Everything I tried either tasted terrible or had too many carbs.

Some protein powders almost

worked but didn't produce quite the right texture. Still, I could feel I was getting closer.

After seven years, I finally found the right combinations and the "Zero Carb Waffle" was born.

Discovering this recipe was like opening my morning to bird songs and perpetual sunshine. Sweet, "bready" and coffee friendly...this find turned out to be a gourmet chameleon.

It could taste like Mom's cinnamon toast, or a crispy cookie-- and even transformed into a walnut-maple delight.

When I tasted my first whipped cream and fresh strawberry waffle sandwich, I felt like I'd been handed the keys to Opulence Island.

I knew I was halfway there.

The next dilemma was unearthing a sweetener.

Health should be the first priority when we consider food. However, because excess weight is a danger to the body, it's all too easy to adopt unhealthy eating regimes. "I'll only do this until I get the weight off," I often told myself.

That rationale left me with headaches, nausea and a carcinogenic phobia as I ingested artificial sweeteners in everything from drinks to frozen desserts. That seemed to be my only option until I at last lit upon two safe sweeteners.

Sucralose, although not carbohydrate-free, was my favorite find for sweetening up my world of diet deprivation. This sweetener has 18 carbs per cup, which is certainly lower than regular sugar. The best news is that so far, research has shown it to have no harmful side effects.

Stevia is a natural herbal sweetener that can be

used for many sweetening purposes. At first I was turned off by its licorice taste, but have since found delicious ways to use it.

These key ingredients are discussed at length in the next section of the book.

The building blocks were finally all in place. Then it was time to hit the kitchen for creating, critiquing, and heavenly consumption.

The results of this satisfying quest are yours to enjoy.

Stocking the Kitchen

• Ingredients •

Low-Carb Ingredients

Everyone has heard of flour, sugar and fat-- the key ingredients in almost all sweets.

In this book, we replace that terrible trilogy with ingredients that are healthier, low in carbohydrates and yet still produce delicious results.

In order to make these recipes, you will need a few items that may be newcomers to your kitchen.

Some may be a little more expensive than the normal trio of fat builders, but they are still a real bargain when compared to pre-packaged low-carb items available in stores. I have tried one terrible tasting low-carb bar that cost a whopping $2.99.

It's a cost cutter's dream to discover that a whole batch of the "Easy Almond Biscotti" can be made for about three bucks.

Most of these desserts are so loaded with protein, they can make a satisfying, high-protein meal replacement. Two biscotti have more protein than two eggs. (Of course, we aren't recommending this as a steady diet.)

These special ingredients are generally available in supermarkets, health food stores or on the Web. It's good to keep an extra supply of ingredients on hand, so you can quickly create your favorite treats when the cravings kick in.

• Protein Powders •

The most important component in this new approach to making desserts is replacing flours and other grains with protein powders and bulking items like psyllium and flaxseed meal.

There are dozens of protein powders on the market, but it's vital to discern the differences.

The protein powders we use contain either zero or low carbohydrates.

Try to keep the protein powders below 10 grams of carbohydrates per cup or 2 grams per tablespoon. Most soy protein powders contain zero carbohydrates. Vanilla whey protein powder usually can be found with less than 10 carbs per cup or 1.5 carbs per tablespoon. Be sure to read the labels.

2/Tblsp = 32/cup.

There are new protein powders that come in a variety of flavors. Vanilla seems to be the most versatile flavor but we use chocolate powder, too. They are usually presweetened, which reduces the amount of low-carb sweeteners required for the recipes. Since each brand has a unique formula, it helps to taste the powder to determine its sweetness.

We use mainly soy and whey protein powders. They each have their unique applications and effect on the taste and texture of the goodies.

I have bought the same type of protein powder by various manufacturers and was amazed by the difference in flavors. For instance, one chocolate whey powder had a rich strong flavor while another brand had barely a whisper of chocolate. It had a definite effect on the outcome of the recipe. It may take a little experimenting to get the right products, but we find that most "failed batters" can be turned into a delicious waffle.

1. Soy Protein Powder

For most baked goods, I use soy protein powder. Because we use a great quantity of protein powders in these recipes, soy is generally the best because it is versatile and less expensive. Just make sure to buy soy protein powder-- not soy flour.

For most recipes I use the zero carb vanilla flavor powder which often contains sweeteners and products that help digest protein, like papaya and other enzymes. These powders can be obtained for as little as five dollars a pound.

Another soy protein powder I find useful is unflavored soy protein isolate. It's similar to regular soy protein powder but contains no additives like sweeteners and flavorings. This is good for piecrusts or other recipes not requiring a sweet taste. (You can also use it for baking breads.)

Soy protein powders are processed from

the bean of the soy plant and have most of the fiber and carbs removed. It is touted to be helpful for relieving symptoms of female hormonal changes and reducing the risk of cardiac problems. The FDA has approved a claim that 25 grams of soy protein daily (in a diet low in saturated fat and cholesterol) may reduce the risk of heart disease.

Soy is not the highest quality protein but the eggs, in most of our recipes, help fill in some of the missing amino acids.

The positive points of soy protein powder are that it is inexpensive and usually contains no carbohydrates.

The comparison chart below shows how well soy protein powder scores when compared to common and highly touted, whole wheat flour. The only area it is lacking in is fiber, and we include loads of additional fiber in almost all the recipes.

<u>Soy Protein Powder</u> vs. <u>Whole Wheat Flour</u>		
Amount: 1 cup	<u>Soy</u>	<u>Wheat</u>
Calories	290	407
Protein	69 grams	16 grams
Carbohydrates	0 grams	87 grams
Fat	3 grams	2.2 grams

2.Whey Protein Powder

A powerful protein powder with many applications is the type made from the by-product of cheese making-- whey. It is known for reducing fat, building muscle, and is considered the highest quality protein on the planet.

It has a 104 B.V. (biological value), which makes it much higher than any animal protein. Surprisingly enough, it is very low in lactose. There are even some types (like whey protein isolate) that have all the lactose removed.

Whey protein digests quickly, so it can relieve hunger faster than other protein powders. However, it doesn't maintain a sustained feeling of fullness so you might feel hungry sooner than with other proteins.

What makes whey protein superior is the branched-chain amino acids that support insulin-like growth factors. Those growth factors are said to have a significant effect on keeping the body slim and youthful.

We find this to be a wonderful product for making cookies, candies and toppings. It is about twice the cost of soy protein powders, but some stores carry a 5-pound jar of whey isolates at a price that works out to about $6.50 a pound.

3. Milk Protein

This slow digesting powder keeps you

full longer and has a higher glutamine content than any other protein powder. That makes it very good for bodybuilding and lean muscle growth.

Although it is a milk product, it is low in lactose. We generally don't recommend this product in our recipes, unless it's in combination with egg protein.

4. Egg Protein

The whites of eggs were once considered the highest standard for protein powders but are now surpassed by whey.

The powder has a slightly bitter taste but has an excellent amino acid profile. It is especially rich in sulfur. It seems to have the best applications when mixed with milk proteins. If one is allergic to milk and soy, egg white protein powder is the perfect choice.

5. Gelatin

Unflavored gelatin is another protein additive that is widely available in the baking section of supermarkets under the name Knox gelatin. For economy's sake, you can often buy or special order gelatin in health stores.

It is sold by the pound and the reduction in price is considerable. A pound lasts a long time and costs around seven dollars. Gelatin is an animal protein and is especially useful for the joints, hair and nails. In this book it is used to thicken shakes, glazes and mousses. When dissolved in water, it is colorless and tasteless.

• Fiber •

I can't imagine a low-carbohydrate lifestyle without some of the fabulous fiber products we use in our recipes. Our bulking agents put elimination on a fast track and help clean the essential byways of the body. These fibers are inexpensive and worth their weight in platinum.

With this increase in fiber, it is vital to drink at least eight glasses of water daily.

1. Psyllium

One key ingredient in many recipes is psyllium husks. The husks are the outer layer of the psyllium seed, which is ground to a coarse powder that is virtually tasteless and gives baked goods a satisfying and essential fiber boost.

Psyllium is a Godsend for an eating style that lacks the roughage found in most fruits, vegetables and grains. Psyllium not only adds a lot of texture to foods, but also cleans the body like a good coarse broom.

It comes in different sizes, but I usually buy it by the pound for around five dollars. The product is commonly called psyllium husks, ground psyllium or colon cleanse.

Psyllium has carbohydrates, but the body doesn't absorb them because the husks are too hard to break down. This wonderful fiber adds texture to cookies, cakes and waffles.

Be sure to use psyllium husks and not the whole seed. I recommend keeping psyllium refrigerated.

2. Flaxseed Meal

This wonderful seed is eaten whole or ground into a meal that is rich in fiber and the essential omega 3 and 6 fatty acids. This fabulous fiber not only adds bulk to our delicious recipes, but studies have shown the seeds to be a powerful and natural way to control cholesterol.

Flaxseed meal is lower in carbohydrates than psyllium, and the health benefits make it priceless. The fibrous makeup of the meal makes the carbs indigestible.

It is important to use flaxseed meal and not the whole seeds for baking.

This meal should be refrigerated. I would also advise buying it in a vacuum-sealed container. It usually costs less than five dollars a pound.

If you have the time, you can buy the fresh seeds and grind them yourself.

Flax

• Sweeteners •

Health should be the top priority when considering an eating plan, but many times we eat things we know are unhealthy while thinking, "I'll only do this until the weight comes off." Therefore, we rationalize feeding our bodies things that are unhealthy at best and carcinogenic at worst.

The biggest dilemma I faced, in writing a low-carb sweets book, was deciding on a sweetener. I tried every product on the market, but it wasn't until recently that better sweeteners became readily available. In this section we will discuss several of the low-carb sweeteners used in our recipes.

1. Sucralose

At last the perfect tasting sweetener--sucralose. This product is available under the trade name Splenda.

Sucralose is a recent FDA approved sweetener that, so far, hasn't had any reported side effects. Oddly enough, it is actually made from sugar. Some clever scientists have managed to change the molecular structure of sugar and come up with a product that has minimal carbohydrates, is low in calories and doesn't promote tooth decay.

Unlike aspartame, it doesn't lose its

sweetening effect when used at high temperatures. So, that makes it great for baking, making candies and dozens of other desserts.

I have tried this product in numerous recipes and I'm delighted with the results. This is not a zero-carb sweetener, however. One cup has 18 grams of carbohydrates.

It is still a sugar, but its lack of nutritional value is offset by its numerous beneficial attributes.

A downside of sucralose is that it is expensive. It costs over three dollars for a 1.9-ounce box of the precious powder. That amount is "supposedly" equivalent to the sweetness of one pound of regular sugar. We use the kind that pours like granulated sugar, not the individual tiny packages.

If you want to convert a favorite recipe to a low-carb version, I suggest replacing a cup of sucralose for every cup of sugar.

I try to use mainly sucralose in my recipes. For the sake of convenience, most recipes call for sucralose as a sweetener. However, there is a 'sweetness conversion chart' at the end of this section if you want to substitute other sweeteners.

2. Stevia

Stevia is a natural herbal sweetener that definitely has some valuable applications for dessert making. It is often used in commercial products like protein bars and drinks.

This sweetener is made from a plant that grows throughout Latin America and parts of the southwestern United States. It has been used for over a hundred years as a sweetener in Japan and South America.

Stevia has 30 times the sweetness of sugar but has negligible calories and carbohydrates.

Besides being a sweetener, it has other valuable properties. A report from the Hiroshima University School of Dentistry reveals that this herb actually suppresses dental bacteria growth rather than feeding it as sugars do.

Other studies have shown a beneficial relationship between stevia and the regulation of blood sugar levels.

Latin American and Japanese scientists also claim that this "all purpose root" works as a tonic, diuretic and can help with mental and physical fatigue.

Stevia's sweetness is not affected by heat (as is aspartame) so it can be used in cooking and baking.

At first I couldn't stand the licorice-like taste, but I found it could be disguised when combined with other flavors like chocolate.

I accidentally came upon a wonderful discovery. By putting a whole vanilla bean in a container of stevia, the licorice flavor almost disappeared and blossomed into a new palatable and fragrant sweetener. It can be used to sprinkle on waffles, bake in desserts and is a great sweetener for lemonade.

I prefer the white powder but it also comes in a liquid form.

3. Aspartame

Although aspartame (commonly called Equal) is found in many diet products, people have reported negative side effects associated with this sweetener.

I sometimes use small amounts of aspartame in recipes that don't require cooking, like shakes, candies and icings. It is less expensive than sucralose and a small amount doesn't seem to have the same negative effects.

Aspartame doesn't maintain its sweetness when heated so it should not be used for baking or cooking.

4. Saccharin

Saccharin is another option when looking for a low-carb sweetener. This is not an ideal product but it has its good points as a sweetening ingredient. It doesn't lose its sweetness in the heating process and is quite inexpensive. I occasionally use the brown sugar flavored saccharin for some goodies. However, it can't be sprinkled on baked goods or waffles, as it tends to taste bitter.

A combination of all the sweeteners can be successfully used in many of the recipes. I prefer stevia and sucralose mixed together.

Sweetness Conversion Chart

1 cup of sucralose = 1 cup sugar

7 teaspoons of stevia = 1 cup sugar

8 teaspoons of saccharin = 1 cup sugar

8 teaspoons of aspartame = 1 cup sugar

• Oils, Nuts & Seeds •

We are just coming out of the "fear of fat" era and happily we have scientific evidence that "good fats" like safflower, olive, canola and nut oils are actually beneficial for the skin, heart, brain and slimming programs.

It has been a real fact-finding mission to gather information that separates the health facts from the myths.

We have definitely been given the thumbs up when it comes to healthy oil but there is one factor that can take any oil and turn it into a dangerous ingredient-- heat. That is why it is imperative that all oils, seeds and nuts be stored in the refrigerator. It is even wise to keep olive oil refrigerated. If it becomes solidified, just run it under hot water for a few minutes and it will liquify.

Left at room temperature, open containers of cooking oils can begin to turn rancid in one week. Rancid foods are linked to increased heart disease and cancer.

I recommend buying cold-pressed oils in opaque glass bottles. Light is another element that can deteriorate the integrity of oils.

1. Butter

Is Butter better? Since most gourmet baking books use butter as the queen of fats, I include butter in many of the recipes.

Because this favorite fat is carbohydrate free, it seems reasonable to call butter an optimal ingredient.

However, because there are many oils with important health properties (and since health is still our main concern) I usually make adjustments if a recipe calls for a great deal of butter. I either substitute half the butter with healthy oils or use part lecithin and oil.

Everyone's body and taste buds responds differently, so experiment and see what combinations work best for you.

2. Lecithin Granules

Lecithin is a long respected supplement that is included in many of the recipes. I love it for its light texture and the health giving properties it adds to baked goods. In our recipes we use lecithin granules.

Lecithin can be used to reduce the need for saturated fats that are found in most baked goods. It also acts as a preservative and has endless beneficial properties.

The lecithin granules we suggest are derived from soybeans. Many health experts recommend including lecithin in one's diet every day.

My favorite health manual, "Prescription for Nutritional Healing," recommends taking 2 tablespoons of lecithin granules daily to help remove cholesterol and lipids from the body.

Lecithin is a fatty substance that acts like an emulsifier and is needed by every living cell in the human body. It is best known for its protection of the brain and heart.

It is a boon to any slimming program because it helps remove fat that is stored in more obvious places like the hips and stomach.

You can find lecithin in health food stores, but it is extremely important that you purchase a product that is fresh and protected from heat and light. All fats are dangerous when rancid, so make sure the lecithin is odor free and tasteless. I recommend buying the granules in a foil-lined cardboard container that is vacuum sealed. Once it is opened, be sure to store in the refrigerator.

3. Nuts

Almost all nuts and seeds can be a wonderful addition for creating low-carb sweets. (Except cashews and peanuts which are both high in carbohydrates.)

In the beginning, I was concerned about the health implications of baking with nuts. My fears were banished when I came across the following information about walnuts.

In a study published in the Annals of Internal Medicine, researchers from Loma Linda University in California and the Hospital Clinic of Barcelona placed 50 men and women with high cholesterol levels on a Mediterranean diet for six weeks. This was followed by another six-week diet in which walnuts replaced 35% of the monounsaturated fat intake. All other variables stayed the same-- the amount of saturated fats, the calories and nutritional qualities of the diet.

Although the Mediterranean diet significantly lowered cholesterol levels, the walnut diet produced even more significant results. According to researcher Emilio Ross, M.D., "If you eat a handful of walnuts a day, you will lower your blood cholesterol and, therefore, lower your cardiovascular risk."

So we happily include a variety of nuts in many of the recipes in this book. Once again, we give the same warning that we gave with oils. Shelled nuts should only be used when fresh and refrigerated. Buy nuts in markets that have a high product turnover. Look at the expiration dates on prepackaged nuts and request that health food stores keep nuts refrigerated. An important deciding factor for freshness is the smell and taste test. If it has a rancid odor or taste, return it to the store.

4. Seeds

We use several types of seeds in our recipes. They contain important essential oils and add flavor and texture.

Flaxseeds and flaxseed meal are essential ingredients in several recipes. Flaxseeds add bulk and important nutrients that are not readily available in other foods. In addition to being nutritious, they are a boon to the elimination system. I find flaxseeds gentler and even more beneficial than psyllium.

My friend Judith Mack (who has beautiful skin and hair) grinds them in an electric grinder and eats them as a breakfast cereal.

I don't use flaxseed oil in baked goods because of its strong taste and inability to withstand high temperatures.

However, flaxseed meal is my favorite booster for cookies, cakes, muffins, waffles and pancakes. Psyllium and flaxseed meal are interchangeable.

Flaxseed meal and psyllium are discussed at length in the fiber section.

Seeds that I like in baked goods are pumpkin, poppy and sunflower. They also make a delicious snack when toasted in a pan and sprinkled with soy sauce and cayenne pepper.

The important thing to remember about all nuts and seeds is to keep them refrigerated. In fact, try to purchase seeds in stores where they are kept cool or sold in vacuum-sealed containers.

Sunflowers

• Flavorings •

The essence of low-carb baking lies in the flavors rather than an overly sweet taste. We enrich the taste with such tempting delights as exotic vanilla beans, dark chocolate and cinnamon. We also use a lot of citrus zest, finely grated peel of lemons, oranges and limes. Occasionally we use an imitation flavor (like maple flavoring) if the real item is too laden with carbohydrates.

Another wonderful flavor enhancer is liquor. We find that brandies, rums and whiskies are an elegant low-carb addition to desserts. They are rich in flavor and, even if you are a teetotaler, the alcohol evaporates in cooking.

1. Vanilla

After a trip to Tahiti, I discovered the wonder of using fresh vanilla beans. The long dark pods initially intimidated me, but I have fallen in love with the enchanting fragrance-- and using them turns out to be quite simple. Just slice the bean lengthwise (it should be soft and pliable) and scrape out the sticky lining inside the skin. Use this dark fragrant part for flavoring anything from baked goods to drinks.

The skins add a wonderful flavor and fragrance in a canister of coffee beans or a bowl of sweetener. You can also use the beans for creating exotic ice teas and drinks.

2. Chocolate

Chocolate is probably the world's favorite flavoring. Satisfying the craving for this sensuous treasure has sent explorers scurrying around the world since antiquity.

We use forms of chocolate in many recipes for an indulgence in taste but not carbohydrates.

- <u>Chocolate Whey Protein Powder</u>

This wonderful powder boosts taste and nutrition to the sky without breaking the carbohydrate bank. We use powders with a carb count of two grams a tablespoon or ten carbs a cup.

- <u>Unsweetened Cocoa Powder</u>

This very accessible powder is found in the baking section of grocery stores. Check the different powders to find the lowest carb count.

- <u>Unsweetened Baking Chocolate</u>

This versatile product is available in half-pound packages and contains eight foil-wrapped bars. Each bar is an ounce and contains four grams of carbohydrates.

- <u>Semi-sweet Chocolate Chips</u>

This is the only ingredient we use that contains some sugar. One third cup of chips contains about 18 grams of carbs. Because these chips are so readily available and easy to use, we justify using them-- as long as the carb count of each goodie falls below five grams.

3. Fruit Flavorings

We are blessed to be living in a time when there are fruit flavorings available in low-carbohydrate products. I particularly like some flavors of Crystal Light drinks to use in icings, shakes, and even some baked goods. Many of the flavors are natural and, because the amount we use is so minuscule, we can risk a small amount of artificial ingredients and sweetener.

4. Imitation Maple Flavoring

This is another discovery that has turned out to be a wonderful low-carb addition to the spice cabinet. Maple flavoring can be used to make syrup or add a "homey" flavor to cookies, pancakes or waffle batters. This product maintains its flavor through high temperatures.

5. Extracts

I was delighted by the variety of extract flavors available for low-carb creations. It is fun to visit a gourmet shop and check out some of the interesting bottles of extracts like pineapple, coconut and even raspberry.

6. Brandy and Liquors

Various recipes call for brandy to flavor

candy, cookies and cakes. I have been pleased with the taste of this elegant ingredient. Of course, use a carbohydrate counter before adding anything to a recipe. If you do not want to use alcohol, the good news is that the alcohol evaporates in the cooking process. You can also use imitation brandy and rum flavorings.

7. Coffee

Coffee is a low-carb flavor booster for shakes, icings and baked goods. You can use coffee crystals or strong brewed coffee. I usually keep a jar of brewed coffee in the refrigerator. It's good for an instant shake or as a flavor boost to puddings, cakes or cookies. Coffee adds no carb count to recipes.

8. Vitamin C Crystals

Vitamin C crystals add a delicious tangy flavor to icings, shakes and baked goods like cheesecake. It can make a healthy lemon substitute. The crystals are usually sold in a half-pound jar for under ten dollars. They are a great nutrition booster, with ½ teaspoon yielding 2000 units of vitamin C.

Vitamin C is noted for helping to replace some of the nutrients lost by drinking coffee and using artificial sweeteners.

Saving Money

Making your own low-carb sweets can be a real budget saver. The average recipe costs a fraction of the price of buying low-carb items in stores or restaurants. (If you can even find them.)

One catalog company advertises a low-carb brownie mix for $8.99 a can that produces 18 brownies. Ingredients for our brownie recipe costs about $2.49.

Many protein bars cost more than two dollars, which is the total cost for making a whole batch of waffles. Our goodies also taste better, have more protein and much more fiber.

I now find that I spend less money eating out. If I get hungry while shopping or travelling, I can rely on a few low-carb snacks tucked away in my purse.

These new sweets help you avoid convenience stores, too. I used to go in those stores feeling hungry, and come out with roasted nuts which were marginal in freshness and usually unsatisfying.

Now you can save money for the things you really want. Why not splurge on a dreamy wardrobe for the slimmer new you?

Ready to Dive In?

Tricks of the Treats

KitchenTools
Make the Job Easier

Creating low-carb sweets can be a quick and easy job if you have the right tools. We will highlight a few favorites that help make preparation a pleasure instead of a chore.

For the seasoned homemaker, these products are probably kitchen staples-- but we feel it is important to make this book novice friendly, too.

1. Food Processor

A food processor is my favorite tool for creating these recipes. It not only mixes dough, chops nuts, and whips egg whites, but it can also be used for making ice cream.

An 11-cup machine is big enough to tackle any job we might present it.

It's not necessary to blow the budget on a brand new top-of-the-line model. I bought my Cuisinart at a thrift store for fifteen dollars. I have used it almost every day for five years and the motor is as strong as the day I bought it.

You can also find used food processors in the small appliance section of the newspaper. Yard sales are also a good place to score a food processor or you might check on the Web. Oftentimes someone's "good intentions" become a guilt- provoking item taking up space in the kitchen... so ask friends if they have one that's become a dust catcher.

If you have never used a food processor, fear not. I was terrified of my machine when I first brought it home. However, once I learned how to open and close the lid, it's easier than an ATM.

Although it often comes with many blades, I use the metal propeller-shaped blade for all the recipes. Experiment and see what works best for you.

2. Mixer

A self-standing or hand mixer is another useful product. I have an inexpensive hand mixer that works well for mixing light batters, beating eggs and whipping cream.

Of course, you can also use a whisk if you are into a more orthodox style. That's a great workout, too.

3. Blender

A blender is helpful for making shakes, purees, whipped cream, and meringues. A machine with a strong motor is best; you can use the extra power to create frappe coffee drinks and crush ice.

I don't have a powerful blender, so I just turn the machine off and on frequently to prevent the motor from burning out.

4. Waffle Iron

A waffle iron is probably going to become one of your most used kitchen tools. I use mine every day and it's a real work-horse for such a small investment.

I recommend the non-stick Belgian iron, but any kind works well. You often see new waffle makers on sale for less than twenty dollars.

5. Baking Pans and Cookie Sheets

You will need baking pans and cookie sheets.   I'm sure everybody has a few of these in the kitchen. A good substitute for an expensive cake pan is to unscrew the handle of a heavy-duty, non-stick frying pan and use it for any baked desserts. You will never have to scrub again-- even sticky coffee cake comes out easily.

Good cookie sheets are nice, but we find any sheet pan lined with aluminum foil, waxed paper or parchment paper makes cleanup a snap.

6. Pan Liners

Now for my second favorite kitchen helper-- pan liners. Liners like parchment paper are a miracle on a roll. This 11-inch wide paper is used to line cake pans, cookie sheets and, in a pinch, I have put it directly on the oven rack lined with foil.

Nothing sticks to it and the price is usually only pennies an application.

I felt like I had won the lottery when I found out you can make your own parchment paper by coating white typing paper with cooking oil.

While perusing through some old cookbooks, I was delighted to discover that waxed paper can also be used to line pans. Just be certain to keep oven temperatures no higher than 350°.

Whatever form of liner you use, it's a real boon for making everything from cookies to coffee cakes.

Another plus point is that it reduces the amount of oil needed to prevent baked goods from sticking to the pans.

So, don't worry if you can't afford expensive baking equipment-- paper liners are the "fairy Godmothers" of kitchen gear.

Other paper items I love are cupcake liners and paper candy cups. The cupcake papers are available in most grocery stores and it's easy to find the papers for candy in gourmet shops. These two products make a big splash for little cash.

Parchment Paper

7. Citrus Grater

Many of the recipes call for grated lemon, lime or orange peel. The finely grated colored rind is commonly called zest. There is a small tool created specifically for making the job a lot more appealing. Citrus graters are found in gourmet shops or look up a source on the Web.

Easy Cleanup
Less Work - More Play

Facing a sink full of messy dishes can be a huge barrier to getting in the kitchen and creating your favorite treats. We have a few tips to make the job easier.

1. Hire a housekeeper - just kidding.
   - or -
2. Work smart.

Since the food processor is the machine that is used the most, I recommend oiling or spraying non-stick coating on the blade and bowl to save a lot of cleanup time.

Another important tip is to never leave the batter in the bowl for more than a few seconds.

As soon as the batter is mixed, put it directly in the pan, waffle iron or storage bowl. Then, while the batter is baking in the pan or waffle iron, rinse and wash the bowl by hand or put it in the dishwasher.

If you are really busy and can't stop to cleanup, just put a few inches of water and liquid detergent in the work bowl and run the machine until you have soap bubbles up to the top. Then when you find time, it won't be as hard to clean.

The blender is another favorite tool that can be almost self-cleaning. Try making a habit of the following procedure: as soon as the blender is empty, add about two inches of water and a squirt of liquid detergent. Put it back on the motor and let run until soap bubbles reach the top. Then just rinse with really hot water and let air dry.

We have mentioned the wonderful attributes of using parchment paper and other pan liners in "Tools to Make the Job Easier." Those wonderful liners make cleaning pans a piece of cake.

Work smart, so you have the time to do the things that bring you real pleasure.

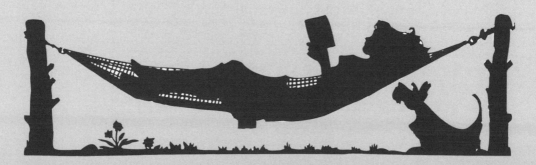

• Plan Ahead •
Make It Easy On Yourself

If we want to be prepared for any occasion (travel, parties or that dreaded "if I don't eat something sweet I'll come unglued") it is important to plan ahead.

In other words, no matter what comes up, we are going to have the food or the supplies we need to make our favorite sweets.

Otherwise, my tale of woe might be yours.

Just the other day, I was so busy working on my book that I hadn't taken the time to make any low-carb goodies. I hurried off to work, grabbing a bottle of water and hoping for the best.

It turned out to be one of those killer workdays, crowded freeways and everything taking longer than usual. I ended up in a real time crunch. I was really hungry but only had ten minutes to eat. Definitely not enough time to go to a restaurant for a chicken salad.

Ordinarily I would have pulled out a snack from my purse and enjoyed a few cookies with a cool drink.

Instead, I bought a coffee and biscotti at a coffee bar. I ended up with a real blood sugar let down, started craving sweets and blew a whole day of my "get slender plan."

That's why I always try to make a big

batch of my favorite sweets and keep it sealed in the refrigerator.

I always bring along treats whenever I travel. I have a purse-sized cooler that's filled with tasty snacks to eat in the airport or on the plane. Otherwise, I might get tempted to eat the delicious airplane treats. Ha!

When we went to Canada for a family visit, I made enough coffee cake for the week. I wrapped it tightly and stored it in my suitcase. When we arrived at the house, I just popped my treats in the refrigerator. In the morning when everyone else was eating Mom's delicious "Morning Glory Muffins," I had my coffee cake and felt privileged. The only hard part was keeping everyone out of my stash.

My very favorite travel food is "Heavenly Almond Cookies." They last for a week, don't have to be refrigerated and are high in protein and fiber.

While travelling in Tahiti I had a giant catastrophe. The humidity was so high that my week's worth of munchies became moldy. The whole situation was saved by an emergency can of easy-mixing protein powder I had packed in my suitcase.

I simply mixed vanilla shakes in the hotel room until we got to our friends' house. Then, I delighted our hosts with a quickly made up recipe of "Tahitian Lemon Crepes." Everyone loved them. They had no idea I was making an emergency move to save myself

Make cookies for trip!

from breakfasts of croissants or French baguettes.

On the home front, I always keep a batter of my favorite waffles in the refrigerator. Even my lanky husband loves these treats. Of course, I put yogurt, fruit and nuts on his. I never feel deprived with a waffle that's topped with nuts, sweetened cinnamon and butter.

The point I am trying to make is that it's mandatory to always keep a cache of treats and essential supplies on hand.

If you do get so busy that you find the cookie cupboard bare, with the help of a food processor, you can put together a waffle batter in the same amount of time it takes to boil water.

If you only have one hour a week to prepare low-carb sweets, I would first make a double recipe of one of your favorite take-along treats. Then, while the food processor is out and the goodies are baking, prepare the cookie dough of your choice. Wrap the dough in plastic and store in the refrigerator for those emergency "cookie cravings."

Give the food processor one more job and make up a waffle batter. Store that in the fridge, too.

With a little planning, you are free to sail off into your life with a refrigerator full of treats and meals.

Keeping these goodies on hand will help you from falling off the path to the body of your dreams.

• Sweet Strategies •
Clever Planning for all Occasions

With a bit of clever planning, we won't get trapped in any social situation. Some of the following tactics can safely guide us through any affair with grace and ease.

The Holidays

Those jolly holly days can be a real trial unless we keep a few pleasure principles in mind. With temptations abounding, we must get in the kitchen and rustle-up the most elegant treats. Special goodies that we usually don't take the time to create. I love splurging on cream puffs that are crowned with chocolate. Macadamia Fudge always puts me over the top of the indulgence scale. A cheesecake laced with cranberries can start me humming, "Deck the Halls."

Parties can become a breeze if we volunteer to bring a salad and dessert. With this strategy, we will be guaranteed a healthy treat to accompany any main dish and the desserts is usually something chocolate, elegant and loaded with whipped cream!

This plan will make you a hero with other guests, too-- especially when you reveal the carb count.

Espresso Yourself

Just try to get something low-carbohydrate in a trendy coffee bar. I treat myself by bringing my own delicious cookies or brownies to savor while sipping my favorite cup of java. It doesn't matter that my mate is eating an espresso brownie or that the person at the next table is having mocha fudge cake. My goodies are not only delicious but also helping me create my "perfect body." Life is good.

The Movies

This is a hard one. I love popcorn but a delicious box of those hot morsels of crunchiness is out of the picture. Deprivation? Certainly not. I just tote along my "Made in the Shade Lemonade" in a "to-go" cup and a few pieces of "Macadamia Fudge."

Since many theaters charge $9 admission, they can survive without my popcorn purchase.

Visiting the "Feed Freak"

Many of us know this saga: The infamous visit to mom, auntie or anyone else whose slogan is "Eat-Eat."

Many times, that host is the very one who inadvertently helped create our girth in the first place. It seems that no matter how carefully I explain my diet, that person just doesn't get it. But I have learned to never eat anything just to please.

I created a three-part response for any troublesome food invitations:

- I eat nothing that isn't low-carb, not even a bite. I respond that I only want salad (or veggies) and any kind of protein.
- I tell my host that I love her, appreciate her, but ask if she doesn't want me to be healthy and beautiful?
- I give her a big kiss, when she says that I am beautiful, and then pull out my low-carb sweets as I finish my meal with a cup of tea or coffee.

No Pity Parties

I love dinner parties but hate to be put in a situation where I feel deprived of indulgences available to other guests. It it's not a potluck party; one of my favorite solutions is to bring the host a low-carb cheesecake. I put it on a pretty plate, give it an over-the-top presentation and then look forward to dessert. The hardest part is getting a piece of the cake before the other guests have eaten everything but the paper doilies.

Deprivation? What deprivation?

The Recipes

Waffles

Cookies

Muffins

Cakes

Pies

Shakes

Ice Cream

Candies

Notes on Taste and Texture:

The possibilities of this ground-breaking approach to the culinary arts are infinite. Now we can create low-carb versions of some of the world's most scrumptious desserts.

Most of the recipes in this book are "original takes" on old standards. Some may have a slightly different taste, texture or sometimes both.

When it comes to taste, I prefer goodies that are on the semi-sweet side and my favorite type of chocolate is bittersweet. If you prefer your indulgences on the high-end of the sweetness scale, just add extra sweetener. (Remember to include the additional carbs into the final count.)

Texture is another factor that figures into dessert preference. To change the texture, altering the length of baking time will have a dramatic effect. For instance, if you want to make cookies crispier, just bake a little longer. The opposite holds true for creating softer types of cookies.

The types of protein powders also change the sweetness and consistency of a dessert. I have been very disappointed when I have perfected a recipe using one brand of protein powder and then used the exact same proportions with another brand and the results were totally different. So remember, if a dessert doesn't meet your standards, be experimental and try a few simple alterations.

We are "pros in the making" on this sweet new turf, so get ready to tee-off towards par excellence treats.

Waffles

Pancakes, Crêpes & Blintzes

AMAZING BUT TRUE
ZERO-CARB WAFFLE

This recipe is so simple and versatile that one can eat waffles every day and still not grow tired of them. This waffle has a bread-like texture that is soul satisfying and enough fiber to make body cleansing a breeze. It's a good idea to keep a container of the batter in the refrigerator for an instant meal.

4 eggs
¼ cup oil
2 cups water
¼ cup lecithin granules
1 cup zero carb soy protein powder

¾ cup psyllium husks
1 tablespoon cinnamon, vanilla extract or imitation maple flavoring
Sweetener to taste (optional)

Preheat waffle iron

- In a large bowl or a food processor, combine eggs, oil, water and lecithin. Mix until frothy.

- Add the remaining ingredients and beat well.

- When waffle iron is ready, add enough batter to cover the inside of the waffle iron with about an inch of room around the perimeter.

- Bake until golden brown.

Yield: 8   Protein: 16 grams   Carbs: 0

Variations

You can add butter and nuts to the waffle iron before putting in the batter.

To make cinnamon nut waffles, put nuts and butter in the waffle batter. When baked, top with butter, more cinnamon and sweetener.

Whipped cream and strawberries makes this a faux strawberry shortcake.

A few blueberries are a delicious addition to this gourmet treat.

VERY VANILLA WAFFLES

These light, delicious waffles are perfect when topped with berries and whipping cream. You might feel like royalty when you sit down to this elegant breakfast meal.

2 cups water
2 eggs
2 tablespoons lecithin granules
2 tablespoons cooking oil
1 teaspoon vanilla extract (or
   scrapings of a vanilla bean)

½ cup psyllium
½ cup flaxseed meal
1 cup vanilla whey protein

Preheat waffle iron

- Combine first 5 ingredients in a food processor or mixing bowl. Beat thoroughly.

- Add dry ingredients and mix well.

- Oil waffle iron using a brush and cooking oil.

- Put batter in middle section of the waffle iron. (They expand.)

- Bake waffles until the cooking indicator light goes off.

- Serve immediately with your favorite topping.

Yield: 6   Protein: 12 grams   Carbs: 2 grams each

The Wonder Waffle

This waffle is a healthy treat for those who can't tolerate eggs or dairy products. It tastes great, has a nice texture, is low in carbohydrates and loaded with fiber.

1½ cups water
¼ cup oil
¼ cup lecithin
½ cup flaxseed meal
¼ cup psyllium husks
⅔ cup soy protein powder
1 tablespoon cinnamon (optional)
1 tablespoon sucralose (optional)

Preheat waffle iron

- Put water, oil and lecithin in a mixing bowl or food processor and mix well.

- Add flax meal and psyllium and mix.

- Blend in the remaining ingredients. The batter is thick.

- Place about 3 or 4 tablespoons across the middle of the waffle iron and let cook until the light signals the waffle is ready. (Each waffle iron has its own mechanism.)

- For a crisper waffle, bake for a few extra minutes.

- Serve with a low-carb maple syrup topping and roasted pecans.

- Nuts and imitation maple flavoring can also be added to the batter.

Yield: 6   Protein: 10 grams   Carbs: 2 grams each

Free-For-All Waffles

I developed this recipe for people who are allergic to dairy, eggs and soy. For those sufferers, we are offering relief from breakfast boredom. This new treat may make one feel brand new. How about a bike ride?

2 cups water
2 tablespoons cooking oil
1 cup flaxseed meal
1 cup psyllium husks
1 tablespoon cinnamon or
   vanilla extract
Sweetener to taste

Preheat waffle iron

- In a food processor or mixing bowl, combine all ingredients until the dry products are mixed in completely.

- Let batter sit for about 10 minutes, so the psyllium and flax meal have a chance to absorb the liquid.

- Coat the waffle iron with non-stick spray or cooking oil.

- I like to let these waffles bake until they are almost crispy, but experiment and find your favorite texture.

Yield: 6   Protein: 1 gram   Carbs: 3 grams each

PECAN PANCAKES

If pancakes are a treat you thought you could never have again, then try these low-carb delights. This recipe can be customized to your taste by adding nuts, maple flavoring, or even a few blueberries.

¾ cup soy flour
Pinch of salt
½ teaspoon baking powder
1 cup water
2 tablespoons oil or melted butter

3 eggs
Sweetener to taste
1 teaspoon vanilla extract
   (or grated lemon peel)
¼ cup chopped pecans

- In a large bowl, combine soy flour, salt, baking powder and sweetener.

- In another bowl, mix water, butter, eggs and vanilla until well combined. Add nuts.

- Stir wet ingredients into dry until mixed but still a little lumpy.

- Heat oiled griddle or pan to a medium temperature.

- Using a ladle or spouted cup, pour enough batter to make a 4 inch pancake.

- When golden brown on bottom, flip and brown other side.

Yield: 12   Protein: 10 grams   Carbs: 1 gram each

PANCAKES SUPREME

Everyone loves pancakes and these jewels are a crowning glory for any morning. The nuts and spice combination make these different from any other flapjack. These cakes are so delicious, it only takes a little butter and low-carb syrup to put these on top of your list of morning favorites.

1½ cups filberts (or favorite nuts)
1½ cups soy protein powder
¾ cup flaxseed meal or psyllium
2 tablespoons sweetener
1 tablespoon cinnamon
2 teaspoons baking powder

1 teaspoon baking soda
1 teaspoon salt
3 large eggs
2 cups water
½ cup melted butter
Cooking oil

Preheat oven to 350°

- Toast nuts until golden brown in a 350° oven.

- If using filberts, remove skins and then place nuts in food processor or blender to chop finely.

- In a large bowl, mix all the dry ingredients together.

- Place all the liquids in a small bowl and whisk until well combined.

- Stir egg mixture into dry ingredients until evenly moistened.

- Add 1¼ cups of the nut mixture to the batter. (Save the rest to top the pancakes.)

- Place a 12-inch non-stick frying pan or griddle over medium heat.

- When heated, add some oil and turn pan to coat evenly.

Maple Syrup

Nothing perks up a pancake like the robust flavor of maple syrup. This recipe has all the taste and few of the carbs so we can feel free to use this favorite flavoring on everything from flapjacks to ice cream.

½ cup boiling water
1 cup sucralose
1 teaspoon unflavored gelatin (optional)
1 teaspoon imitation maple flavor
2 tablespoons soft butter

- Put hot water over the gelatin and stir until completely dissolved.
- Add remaining ingredients and mix until butter is melted.
- Serve immediately and store in the refrigerator.

Yield: 12 tablespoons   Protein: 1 gram   Carbs: 1.5 grams each

- Pour ½ cup of the batter into pan and cook until bottom of pancake is browned and starting to look dry around the edges.
- Turn with a wide spatula and cook for about another 2 minutes.
- Serve immediately with our maple syrup.
- Keep pancakes warm in a 200° oven if not serving immediately.

Yield: 18   Protein: 8 grams   Carbs: 2 grams each

CHERRY PECAN BAKED PANCAKE

Just when you knew you could never wake up to another boring piece of protein, we have come up with a sumptuous breakfast dish that will make your morning.

It will be about 30 minutes from starting to serving, so plan ahead.

¾ cup water
½ cup sucralose
2 eggs
Pinch of salt
Zest of 1 lemon
½ cup soy protein powder
⅓ cup cooking oil

¾ cup chopped pecans
⅓ cup fresh, canned or frozen
   pitted sour cherries
1 tablespoon lemon juice
1 teaspoon cinnamon
2 tablespoons butter

Preheat oven to 425°

- **Combine water, ¼ cup of sucralose, eggs, salt, lemon zest, protein powder and oil in a food processor and beat until frothy. (About 30 seconds.)**

- **In a 10-inch ovenproof or cast-iron skillet, heat the butter over low heat.**

- **Add the pecans and shake the pan to lightly toast the nuts.**

- **Put in the cherries, lemon juice, cinnamon and remaining sucralose. Stir until completely mixed.**

- **Pour the batter over the warm fruit and nuts.**

- **Bake for 20 minutes or until golden brown.**

- **A knife inserted in the middle should come out clean.**

- **Slice into four pieces and serve immediately with butter or whipped cream.**

Yield: 4   Protein: 6 grams   Carbs: 5 grams each

TAHITIAN LEMON PANCRÈPES

While traveling in Tahiti I came up with these tasty little gems. These treats are thinner than a pancake but thicker than a crepe. Everyone loved them and it saved me from a breakfast of carb-laden croissants.

Juice of 2 lemons
3 eggs
1 cup of water
2 tablespoons cooking oil
Scrapings of 1 vanilla bean or
    1 teaspoon vanilla extract

1 cup whey protein powder
1 teaspoon grated lemon peel
(optional)
Sweetener to taste — @ 1 Tblsp.

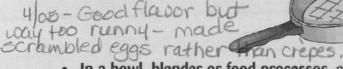

Toppings
① Butter
   Splenda
   Nuts
② Cream cheese +
   lemon juice
      strawberries

4/05 - Good flavor but way too runny - made scrambled eggs rather than crêpes.

- In a bowl, blender or food processor, combine lemon juice and peel, eggs, water and oil.

- Add vanilla, protein powder and sweetener. Blend until lumps are dissolved.

- Heat a frying pan to medium temperature and add enough oil to coat bottom of pan.

- Pour a couple tablespoons of batter into pan and swirl to cover bottom. Cook until almost dry on top.

- Turn pancake over and cook about another minute.

- Spread with butter and sprinkle with sweetener and nuts. Roll into a cigar shape and voila!

- They are wonderful with cream cheese (that's been diluted with sweetened lemon juice) and strawberries.

Yield: 10   Protein: 10 grams   Carbs: 2 grams each

Dessert Crèpes

This crepe recipe produces a wonderful treat with very little effort. You can keep the batter in the refrigerator for several days.

In less than five minutes you can make a couple of crepes and feel like you're on a romantic French vacation.

Imagine sitting in a trendy sidewalk café, sipping espresso, savoring your crepes and thinking "How blessed we truly are."

1 cup water
4 eggs
Pinch of salt

1 cup soy protein powder
3 tablespoons melted butter

- Put water, eggs and salt in a blender or food processor and mix until just combined.

- Add protein powder and blend for 30 seconds. (Don't over mix.)

- If convenient, refrigerate batter for at least 30 minutes. (Overnight is ideal.)

- Melt butter in crèpe pan or small non-stick skillet.

- Pour in about 2 tablespoons of batter.

- Tilt pan to distribute batter evenly.

- Cook about half a minute or until bottom is set and comes away easily from the bottom of the pan. Turn crèpe over by putting a plate on top of the pan and invert. Then slide uncooked side of crèpe onto pan for a minute.

- Put on a dessert plate and top with your favorite filling.

FILLINGS

- Personal palate is the best criteria for deciding what to put on crèpes. The possibilities are endless.

- I personally love whipped cream, strawberries and toasted pecans, rolled up like a cigar.

- Fill crèpe with raspberries, whipped cream and walnuts.

Yield: 10   Protein: 8 grams   Carbs: 1 gram each

Very Berry Blintzes

A cheese blintz brunch is eating in the lap of luxury-- and this recipe creates a slimmer lap, too.

It's a good idea to make the crèpes and filling the night before you serve them. Then in the morning, you only have to fill, fold and fry.

Make extras and freeze them for a convenient meal.

1 cup water
4 eggs
1 cup soy protein powder
Pinch of salt
3 tablespoons melted butter
1 tablespoon sucralose
3 tablespoons butter for frying

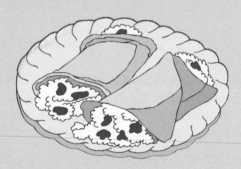

Step One (Crèpe batter):

- Mix water, melted butter and eggs in a large bowl with whisk or an electric mixer.

- Add protein powder, salt, and sucralose. Mix on low speed until the powder is incorporated.

- Put bowl in the refrigerator for at least an hour.

Step Two (Making the crèpe):

- Add butter to coat bottom of a crèpe pan or small skillet that has been heated to a medium temperature.

- When butter is melted, add about 2 tablespoons of the batter and tilt the pan to completely cover the bottom surface.

- Let the crêpe cook for about 30 seconds, or until top is starting to dry.

- Remove crêpe by putting a plate over the pan and flipping the crêpe so the browned side is up. (For blintzes, you only cook crêpes on one side.)

- Continue this process until all the batter is used.

Step Three (Making the filling):

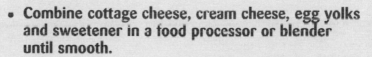

8 ounces whole milk cottage cheese
8 ounces cream cheese (room temperature)
2 egg yolks
1 heaping teaspoon sucralose
1 teaspoon lemon juice
¼ cup berries (optional)
Salt to taste

- Combine cottage cheese, cream cheese, egg yolks and sweetener in a food processor or blender until smooth.

- Stir in lemon juice, berries and salt with a spoon.

Step Four (Making the blintz):

- Spoon a heaping tablespoon of the filling in the middle of the crêpe. Fold both sides inward.

- Melt butter in a non-stick pan over a medium heat. Carefully put crêpes in the pan and fry on both sides until golden brown.

- Topping: Sour cream is the traditional topping for blintzes. A few berries add flavor and color.

Yield: 6   Protein: 12 grams   Carbs: 2.5 grams each

Cookie Caper

Sweet deprivation creates subtle psychological scars, especially in *childhood. It makes one feel "less than."*

To a child it seems that: "Everyone else gets to eat yummy stuff-- except me."

I discovered a helpful solution for getting kids out of this sticky trap. Low-carb sweets are a winning combination for breaking this lock of denial.

A mother of a rotund young daughter, who was suffering ridicule at school because of her weight, reported great success with this novel low-carb sweet approach.

The first step required parent and child having a talk about the child's favorite treat-- cookies. No deep psychological exploration; the mother simply asked what type of cookies the girl liked best and then asked if she would like to help make them. The resounding "yes" let the mother know she was on the right track.

The next step was rolling up their sleeves and hitting the music-filled kitchen for a little cookie klatch.

It took time to come up with the child's ideal cookie but, at last, "Fabulous Fudgies" were given thumbs up.

The mother and daughter both took great pride in this cookie caper.

In fact, the girl was so pleased, she went to school and excitedly showed-off the cookies that **she made herself**. *The girl confessed to her mother that previously she would beg her best friend to trade one Oreo for her bag of baby carrots. (Not happening.)*

The child was carefully taught that all sweets are not created equal. Her healthy treats are different than the sugar-loaded goodies that cause disease, tooth decay and weight gain.

The latest report from the delighted mother is that food battles are a thing of the past and the child has started enjoying more balanced meals. The best news is that the girl's weight has stabilized. As she has grown taller, she is slimming down.

Cookies
Brownies and Bars

CHOCOLATE CHIP DELIGHTS

These heavenly cookies are spiked with chocolate chips, walnuts and a hint of vanilla. They're not only delicious but so easy to make. You can go from conception to confection in less than 30 minutes.

½ cup soft butter
2 eggs
1 teaspoon vanilla extract
1 teaspoon baking soda
¾ cup sucralose
½ teaspoon salt

1 cup vanilla whey protein powder
2 tablespoons flaxseed meal or
   psyllium powder
⅓ cup semi-sweet chocolate chips
1 cup coarsely chopped walnuts

Preheat oven to 375°

- In a large bowl, combine butter, eggs, vanilla and baking soda with an electric mixer or food processor.

- Add sweetener and salt. Mix thoroughly.

- Put in protein powder and flaxseed meal; combine well.

- Add chips and nuts, and mix by hand with a large spoon.

- Drop heaping teaspoons of batter on a cookie sheet.

- Bake 12 minutes, or until golden brown.

- Remove from oven and cool cookies on a wire rack.

Yield: 20   Protein: 6 grams   Carbs: 2 grams each

Maple Pecan Drops

One rainy afternoon, I was craving something sweet but the cookie jar was empty and the cupboard almost bare.

Not wanting to go shopping in the storm, I searched the kitchen and found pecans and maple flavoring to team up for these "sun-provoking" cookies.

½ cup cooking oil
¼ cup soft butter
2 teaspoons imitation maple flavor
1 cup sucralose
2 eggs

1 teaspoon baking soda
Pinch of salt
1 cup soy protein powder
⅓ cup flaxseed meal or psyllium
1 cup chopped pecans

Preheat oven to 375°

- In a large mixing bowl or food processor, blend the oil, butter and sweetener.
- Mix in eggs.
- Add the maple flavoring, baking soda and salt.
- Stir in the flaxseed meal.
- Mix in protein powder.
- Add the pecans.
- Put heaping teaspoons of dough on non-stick cookie sheets.
- Bake for about 10 minutes.
- Turn cookies over and bake until golden brown (about 5 minutes.)
- Let cool on a wire rack before serving.

Yield: 18   Protein: 7 grams   Carbs: 2 grams each

LEMON COOKIES

These delicious cookies have a tangy flavor and loads of sweet satisfaction. They have practically no carbs and lots of fiber, which makes them perfect for the first days of adjusting to a low-carb regime.

4 eggs
3 tablespoons oil
Juice of 2 lemons
2 tablespoons lemon peel
   (finely grated)
2 tablespoons lecithin
   granules

1 cup whey protein powder
½ cup psyllium
1 cup sucralose
1 cup chopped pecans
   (or walnuts)

Preheat oven to 375°

- **In a large mixing bowl (or food processor with a metal blade) combine the eggs, oil, lemon juice, lemon peel and lecithin.**

- **Put in the psyllium and mix thoroughly.**

- **Add the protein powder and sucralose (minus 2 tablespoons) to the batter.**

- **Blend in the nuts.**

- **Put heaping tablespoons of the dough on non-stick cookie sheets. Sprinkle the tops of the cookies with the remaining sucralose. Flatten with a fork.**

- **Bake for about 12 minutes or until golden brown.**

- **Remove cookies from pan and cool on a wire rack.**

Yield: 20   Protein: 6 grams   Carbs: 2 grams each

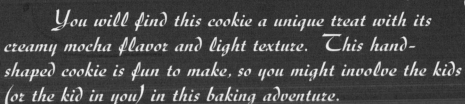

LIGHT AND LUSCIOUS
PECAN JUMBLES

You will find this cookie a unique treat with its creamy mocha flavor and light texture. This hand-shaped cookie is fun to make, so you might involve the kids (or the kid in you) in this baking adventure.

4/04
Very dry
Good flavor

1 cup soft butter	1 teaspoon baking soda
1 egg	¼ teaspoon salt
1 cup sucralose	1 cup soy protein powder
2 teaspoons vanilla	1 cup whey protein powder
extract	1 cup chopped pecans

Preheat oven to 325°

- In a large bowl, mix together the butter, <u>only</u> ¾ cup sucralose, egg and vanilla.

- Completely incorporate the baking soda and salt into the mixture.

- Stir in the protein powders. Add nuts.

- Remove dough from bowl and wrap in plastic. <u>Refrigerate for at least <u>an hour</u></u>.

- Hand shape dough into 1-inch balls and then roll them in a bowl with the remaining sucralose. *Had plenty of sugar, Can roll as a group.*

- Place balls on non-stick cookie sheets and bake for about 12 minutes.

- Transfer to wire rack to cool. *> don't spread much, so can get all on 1 lg sheet at one time*

parchment

Yield: 36   Protein: 6 grams   Carbs: 2 grams each

ALMOST HEAVEN
ALMOND COOKIES

These tasty cookies have the texture of a peanut butter cookie but taste like a Chinese almond cookie. They make a handy travel snack because they stay crunchy and fresh for a long time.

1½ cups raw almonds
2 tablespoons oil
4 eggs
3 tablespoons lecithin granules

2 teaspoons almond extract
1 cup sucralose
1½ cups vanilla soy protein
   powder

Preheat oven to 375°

- Put 1 cup of the almonds and the oil in the bowl of a food processor (or blender); process until mixture is the texture of chunky peanut butter.

- Add the eggs, lecithin, extract, sucralose and the remainder of the almonds. Process until the nuts are coarsely chopped.

- Add the protein powder and mix thoroughly. The dough will become very stiff. (If using a blender, you will want to transfer almond mixture to a large bowl and stir in protein powder by hand.)

- Place heaping teaspoons of dough on non-stick cookie sheets and flatten with a fork.

- Bake for about 12 minutes. Turn cookies over and bake until golden brown (about 3 more minutes.)

Yield: 20   Protein: 7 grams   Carbs: 2 grams each

FABULOUS FUDGIES

*I created these treats one disastrous day when
I was teetering on the edge of a "binge/guilt" abyss.
Holding on by my fingernails-- it took only 20
minutes to make these fabulous cookies and a pot of spice tea.
Soon, the gloom lifted and I was saved from tum-
bling into a vat of Ben and Jerry's.*

10/04 great!

½ cup soft butter
1 cup sucralose
2 eggs
2 tablespoons brandy (or coffee)
2 teaspoons vanilla extract
½ teaspoon salt
1 teaspoon baking soda

3 tablespoons unsweetened cocoa powder
1 cup chocolate whey protein powder
¼ cup flaxseed meal or psyllium
⅓ cup semi-sweet chocolate chips
1 cup chopped walnuts

*Much more moist than usual
lo-carb cookie*

Preheat oven to 350°

- **Combine butter and sucralose in a food processor or mixing bowl.**

- **Add eggs, brandy and vanilla; mix well.**

- **Add baking soda and salt; mix thoroughly.**

- **Mix in cocoa, whey powder and flaxseed meal.**

- **Stir in nuts and chocolate chips with a large spoon.**

- **Put tablespoons of the dough on non-stick cookie sheets and bake for only 10 minutes.**

- **These cookies are delicious while still warm.**

Yield: 18   Protein: 7 grams   Carbs: 3 grams each

THE EASY ALMOND BISCOTTI

These flavorful, crunchy cookies are the ultimate low-carb breakthrough. I was certain that only an Italian-born pastry chef could make biscotti cookies, but we went even further and devised an easier baking method.

Although biscotti means twice baked, we made this a one step process by forming the crescent-shaped cookies by hand.

1 cup whole almonds
½ cup butter
1 tablespoon oil
1½ teaspoons vanilla extract
1 tablespoon grated lemon rind

2 tablespoons lemon juice
1 cup sucralose
3 eggs
1½ teaspoons baking powder
1½ cups soy protein powder

Preheat oven to 300°

- Sprinkle the almonds on a cookie sheet and roast for about 20 minutes or until nuts are golden brown.

- Remove almonds from the oven and raise temperature to 375°.

- In the bowl of a food processor (using a metal blade) pulse the almonds until they are coarsely chopped. (You can also use a blender.)

- Remove the almonds from work bowl and set aside.

- Put butter, oil, vanilla, lemon juice and rind in food processor and mix until just combined. (You can also use a large bowl and an electric mixer.)

- Add sweetener and mix until completely dissolved.

- Beat in eggs, one at a time.

- Add baking powder and thoroughly mix.

- Gradually add the protein powder, using a spatula to scrape the sides. Stir in almonds with a spoon.

- Wrap dough in plastic and refrigerate for 15 minutes.

- Take a heaping tablespoon of the chilled dough and use your hands to shape into a 3-inch-long crescent. Place on cookie sheets, lined with parchment paper. If parchment paper is not available, use non-stick cookie sheets.

- Put in the oven and bake for 15 minutes. Remove from oven and turn cookies over.

- Reduce oven to 350° and return cookies to bake for 20 minutes.

- Turn off heat and leave pans in the oven (with the door open) while cookies cool.

- Store in an airtight container.

Yield: 16   **Protein: 8 grams**   **Carbs: 2 grams each**

Chocolate Walnut Biscotti

This superlative biscotti has a rich chocolate and walnut flavor. The psyllium husks also gives these crunchy treats an added boost of fiber.

1½ cups soy protein powder
½ cup unsweetened cocoa powder
¼ cup psyllium husks
1 cup sucralose
2 teaspoon baking powder

1 tablespoon instant espresso or coffe powder
2 eggs
½ cup soft butter
1 tablespoon vanilla extract
¾ cup coarsely chopped walnuts

Preheat oven to 325°

- **In large mixing bowl, combine the first 6 dry ingredients.**

- **In a second bowl, beat together the eggs, butter and vanilla.**

- **Pour the wet ingredients into the dry ingredients and mix well.**

- **Stir in nuts.**

- **Refrigerate for at least 15 minutes.**

- **Remove from refrigerator and hand form 3-inch crescent shaped cookies. Put on a non-stick or parchment paper-lined cookie sheet.**

- **Bake for 20 minutes. Remove from oven and turn cookies over.**

- **Return the pans to the oven and bake for about 20 more minutes or until cookies become hard and crunchy.**

- **Remove from pan and let cool on a wire rack.**

Yield: 20   Protein: 8 grams   Carbs: 3 grams each

POPPY SEED BUTTER COOKIES

This delicate cookie is tops in flavor and sweet satisfaction. Pressed for time? This cookie can be put together and served in 20 minutes.

10/04
good flavor; a little dry

½ cup soft butter
½ cup sucralose
1 egg
1 teaspoon vanilla extract

¾ cup soy protein powder
2 tablespoons poppy seeds
1 tablespoon grated orange
  or lemon peel

Preheat oven to 375°

- Beat butter and sucralose with food processor or mixer.
- Add egg and vanilla; mix well.
- Mix in protein powder, poppy seeds and grated peel.
- Drop by teaspoons onto a greased cookie sheet.
- Flatten cookies with your fingertips or a fork .
- Bake for 7 minutes.
- Turn over and brown for 3 more minutes.

These do not spread, so can be close together.

Froze well

Yield: 18   **Protein: 6 grams**   **Carbs: 1 gram each**

Chocolate Angel Clouds

These cookies look like puffs of clouds and beautify any dessert tray. Try not to blush when people sing your praises.

1 ounce chilled unsweetened
  chocolate
¾ cup finely chopped filberts
3 large egg whites
1 cup sucralose
1 tablespoon whey protein powder
½ teaspoon cinnamon
½ teaspoon vanilla extract

Preheat oven to 300°

- Finely grate chilled chocolate.

- Grind nuts to a powder. (A food processor works best.)

- With a mixer, beat egg whites and 2 tablespoons of the sweetener until they form stiff peaks.

- Combine remaining sweetener, whey powder, and cinnamon; carefully add to egg whites in 3 increments.

- Fold in the chocolate and nuts.

- Stir in vanilla.

- Line baking sheet with foil, shiny side up.

- Using a teaspoon, drop batter on pan, leaving 2 inches between cookies.

- Bake for 20 minutes.

- Let cool for at least 10 minutes and then peel cookies from foil.

[Note: To prevent meringues from falling, make them only on a dry, sunny day.]

Yield: 30   Protein: 1 gram   Carbs: 2 grams each

COCONUT CHIP COOKIES

Think crunchy, with a splash of melted chocolate, a sprinkling of coconut and you have conjured up a tasteful image of these heavenly delicacies.

1 stick soft butter (4 ounces)
½ cup oil
1 cup sucralose
1 teaspoon maple flavor or
   vanilla extract
3 eggs
1 teaspoon baking soda

¼ teaspoon salt
1½ cups soy protein powder
½ cup dried, finely shredded
   coconut (unsweetened)
1 cup chopped nuts (almonds or
   walnuts)
⅓ cup chocolate chips

Preheat oven to 375°

- In a large bowl, cream the butter, oil and sucralose with a mixer.
- Beat in the maple flavor, eggs, baking soda and salt.
- Mix in the soy powder until totally combined.
- With a large spoon, stir in the coconut, chocolate chips and nuts.
- Put heaping teaspoons of the dough on non-stick cookie sheets.
- Bake in the oven for about 12 minutes.
- Cool on a wire rack.
- Store in an airtight container.

Yield: 20   Protein: 8 grams   Carbs: 3.5 grams each

CHUNKY CHOCOLATE BROWNIES

These brownies are moist, rich and have an extra splurge of walnuts and chocolate chips. They are delicious to the lips and gentle on the hips.

Be Sweet to Yourself

2 squares unsweetened chocolate
½ cup butter
⅔ cup soy protein powder
2 teaspoons baking powder
¼ teaspoon salt

2 eggs
1 cup sucralose
1 teaspoon vanilla extract
1 cup chopped walnuts
⅓ cup chocolate chips

Preheat oven to 350°

- Oil an 8x8x2-inch pan.

- Melt chocolate and butter over boiling water in double boiler or melt in microwave at high setting for about 1 minute.

- Combine dry ingredients in a medium-sized bowl.

- In a large mixing bowl, using a wooden spoon or electric mixer, beat the eggs, sweetener and vanilla extract.

- Stir in chocolate mixture.

- Add dry ingredients and mix thoroughly. Add nuts.

- Spread batter evenly in an 8-inch square pan. Sprinkle chocolate chips on top.

- Bake for 25 to 30 minutes.

- Remove from oven and let cool before cutting into squares.

Yield: 12   Protein: 6 grams   Carbs: 5 grams each

RING YOUR CHIMES

GINGER SNAPPIES

These crunchy cookies are a favorite with those who like their sweets with a bit of spice. A double dose of ginger makes this recipe unique. This dough can be refrigerated for up to 5 days.

½ cup soft butter
1¼ cups sucralose
1 tablespoon imitation maple flavoring
2 egg whites
1 tablespoon grated, fresh ginger
1 teaspoon dried ground ginger

½ teaspoon cinnamon
¼ teaspoon ground cloves
¼ teaspoon salt
1½ teaspoons baking soda
1 cup soy protein powder
¾ cup whey protein powder

10/04 wonderful flavor very dry "like little sponges"*

Preheat oven to 375°

- Use a food processor to beat butter, 1 cup of sucralose, and maple flavoring until fluffy.

- Blend in the egg whites.

- Add fresh ginger, ground ginger, cinnamon, cloves, salt and baking soda. Mix well.

- Put in protein powders and blend thoroughly.

- Put the remaining ¼ cup of sucralose in a small bowl. Drop heaping teaspoons of dough into the sucralose and roll until completely covered. *← use meatball tool*

- Put on non-stick cookie sheet and flatten with a fork. Leave 1½ inches between cookies.

- Bake about 10 minutes.

- Cool on a wire rack.

3/06 - added @2 Tblsp. oil — still very dry.

Yield: ~~50~~ 24   **Protein: 2 grams**   **Carbs: 1 gram each**

← so we tore them in pieces + poured cream over them.

CHOCOLATE CHIP BARS

When it's time to indulge, try these delicious and easy to make delights. The melted chocolate and opulence of walnuts makes this a heavenly treat. It's hard to imagine eating something this delicious-- without guilt.

4 eggs
¾ cup **strong** coffee or water — *cooled*
1 stick soft butter (4 ounces)
½ cup lecithin granules
Scrapings of 1 vanilla bean or 2 teaspoons of vanilla extract
1 cup sucralose

½ cup psyllium or flaxseed meal
1¼ cups low-carb soy protein powder
½ cup semi-sweet chocolate chips
1 cup chopped walnuts

4/05 - good texture; avoids aftertaste, but somewhat bland.

Preheat oven to 400°

- **In a large mixing bowl or food processor, combine the butter, lecithin and sweetener.**

- **Add the eggs, coffee and vanilla. Mix until foamy.**

- **Mix in the protein powder and psyllium.**

- **Add the chocolate chips and walnuts. Thoroughly combine.**

- **Spoon the dough into a large, buttered, 13x9x2-inch baking pan and bake for 25 to 30 minutes.** *23*

- **These bars are delicious to eat when slightly warm and the chocolate is melted.**

Freeze well. Also good next day

Yield: 20   Protein: 7.5 grams   Carbs: 3 grams each

Made ⅔ recipe in Dutch oven — much better. See camping recipes for notes.

Sweet Heart Cookies

These cookies are crunchy, delicious and fun to make. So get out the cookie cutter and make a play date with yourself.

½ cup soft butter
2 tablespoons oil
1½ cups sucralose
2 eggs
1 teaspoon vanilla
Juice from 1 large lemon

1 tablespoon finely grated lemon rind
2 cups soy protein powder
2 teaspoons baking powder
½ teaspoon salt

Preheat oven to 375°

- Mix butter and sweetener until creamy.

- Beat in the eggs, vanilla, lemon juice and rind.

- Combine the powders and salt together; add to the dough and mix well.

- Divide dough in half and wrap in plastic. Chill for 30 minutes.

- Remove dough from fridge and place each piece on sheets of parchment paper cut to the size of the baking pan. Use a rolling pin to flatten dough to about ¼ inch thickness. (If you don't have a rolling pin, flatten with the bottom of a butter-coated glass.)

- Cut out shapes. Remove excess dough from between the shapes. Carefully transfer the parchment (with the cookies still on it) to a baking sheet. Bake until golden brown, about 10 minutes.

- Store leftover dough in the refrigerator for cookies or a piecrust.

Yield: 24   Protein: 8 grams   Carbs: 2 grams each

Orange-Frosted Fudge Brownies

We have taken this decadent frosted brownie from 40 fat-creating grams of carbohydrates down to about 5 grams.

Your taste buds will rejoice and your hips will become slimmer and slimmer.

11/04 very dry

Brownie Ingredients

2 squares unsweetened chocolate
(chopped coarsely)
½ cup butter
1 cup sucralose
2 eggs
2 tablespoons finely grated
orange peel

1 teaspoon vanilla extract
1 cup soy protein powder
1 cup chopped walnuts or
pecans

Preheat oven to 350°

- **Using the high setting of a microwave oven, melt chocolate and butter in a large ceramic bowl for 1 to 1½ minutes. (You can also use a double boiler.)**

- **Remove from heat and add the sweetener, orange peel, vanilla and eggs. Lightly mix with a wooden spoon until just combined.**

- **Thoroughly mix in the protein powder, then add nuts.**

- **Spread the batter in an 8x8x2-inch pan.**

- **Bake for 20 minutes.**

- **Cool before frosting.**

Orange Frosting

some aftertaste

1 8-ounce package of cream cheese
  (low fat is fine)
2 tablespoons finely grated orange rind
1 teaspoon orange extract
  (or 1 tablespoon lemon juice)
½ cup sucralose

Put all the ingredients in a food processor
and thoroughly blend.

- Spread the orange frosting on top of the cooled brownies.

- Be sure to store in the refrigerator because the cream cheese is perishable.

Yield: 9   Protein: 10 grams   Carbs 5.5 grams each

Cakes

PECAN LAYER CAKE

This cake is a beautiful splurge of richness with two scrumptious layers of pecan cake and a luscious lemon cream cheese icing. The batter is primarily made of ground pecans, which create a fabulous flavor and light texture.

Pecan Cake Ingredients

2½ cups ground pecans
4 tablespoons soy protein powder
1 tablespoon baking powder
6 eggs
1 cup sucralose

Preheat oven to 350°

- Grind pecans in a food processor or blender. Set aside.

- Combine eggs and sucralose in a food processor.

- Add the pecans, protein powder and baking powder. Process until the batter is smooth.

- Spread the batter in two 9-inch round, non-stick pans. Bake for 25 minutes. Cakes should be golden brown and springy when lightly touched.

- Remove cakes from the oven and let cool on elevated racks.

Lemon Cream Cheese Icing

8 ounces softened cream cheese
¼ cup butter
2 tablespoons sucralose
Juice of 1 large lemon
1 teaspoon finely grated lemon peel
1 teaspoon vanilla extract

- While the cakes are cooling, make the frosting by beating cream cheese and butter in a small bowl with an electric mixer.

- Mix until fluffy and gradually add sweetener. Beat until smooth.

- Blend in the lemon juice, lemon peel and vanilla.

- When the cakes have cooled, run a knife around side of pan and invert onto a serving plate.

- Spread icing on top of the first layer.

- Put the second layer on the frosted cake and ice the top. (Icing does <u>not</u> go on the sides.) Decorate with pecans.

Yield: 12   Protein: 7 grams   Carbs: 5 grams each

PECAN POUND CAKE

This sumptuous pecan pound cake is a perfect treat, either plain or topped with a low-carb icing.

5 eggs
1 cup sucralose
1¼ cup soy protein powder
¼ cup psyllium

1 teaspoon baking powder
1 cup butter
1 teaspoon vanilla extract
¾ cup pecans

Preheat oven to 325°

- Grease a 9x5x3-inch pan.

- Separate eggs, putting whites in a large bowl.

- Beat the egg whites until they form soft peaks. Add ½ cup of sweetener (a little at a time) and keep beating until stiff peaks are formed.

- Mix together the soy powder, baking powder and psyllium in a medium sized bowl.

- In a larger bowl, using an electric mixer, cream the butter, vanilla and gradually add remainder of the sweetener. Beat until light and fluffy. Add egg yolks (one at a time) and mix well.

- At a low speed, beat in the soy mixture until just combined.

- Stir in the nuts.

- With a wire whisk or rubber scraper (using an under and over motion) gently but thoroughly fold in the egg whites.

- Pour carefully into baking pan.

- Bake 1 hour, or until a toothpick inserted in the center comes out clean.

- Cool in the pan for an hour and then slice into thin pieces.

Yield: 12   Protein: 10 grams   Carbs: 3 grams each

Mocha Cheesecake

Forget lipo-- we can have our cheesecake and slip into our slinkiest clothes. Even the lactose intolerant can enjoy this delicious treat, thanks to the wonderful world of tofu. This cheesecake is creamy faux decadence.

2 cups strong coffee (or water with double strength instant coffee)
4 eggs
1 teaspoon vanilla extract
2 tablespoons plain gelatin
14 ounces soft tofu

½ cup unsweetened cocoa powder
2 tablespoons psyllium
4 tablespoons protein powder
1 cup sucralose
1 cup chopped pecans or walnuts
12 chocolate covered espresso beans (optional)

Preheat oven to 350°

- In large bowl of a food processor, combine coffee, eggs, vanilla and plain gelatin. Blend for a few minutes.

- Add tofu and blend until smooth.

- Put in cocoa powder, psyllium, sweetener and protein powder. Blend until smooth and creamy.

- Pour over a layer of nuts in a 12-inch round pan, lined with parchment paper or foil.

- Bake for 20 minutes.

- Cool and refrigerate for at least an hour before serving.

- Whipping cream and espresso beans are optional toppings.

Yield: 12   Protein: 11 grams   Carbs: 5 grams each

BLACK FORREST CAKE

Want to feel like royalty? Try this magnificent cake. It has a regal presentation and the luscious combination of choco-late and cherry makes this worth the three-step process. Expect your guests' praises as another jewel on your culinary crown.

¾ cup soy protein powder
1 cup sucralose
8 large egg whites at room temperature
3 tablespoons unsweetened cocoa powder
2 teaspoons cream of tartar
1 teaspoon vanilla extract
2 cups water

1 cup unsweetened cherries
  (canned or frozen)
2 teaspoons cornstarch
0.3 ounce package cherry
  gelatin
1 tablespoon brandy
2 cups heavy cream

Preheat oven to 375°

Step 1: Making the cake

- Combine soy powder, cocoa and ½ cup of the sweetener in a bowl.

- In another bowl, use a mixer to beat the egg whites and cream of tartar into soft peaks.

- Add ¼ cup of the sweetener (one tablespoon at a time) and continue beating until egg whites are glossy and stiff.

- Carefully add the protein powder and cocoa to the beaten egg whites in one-third cup increments.

- Put batter in two 8-inch cake pans, lined with parchment paper or foil.

- Bake for 20 to 25 minutes. Cakes should be springy to the touch.

- Turn cake pans upside down and cool on a wire rack.

- While cakes are cooling, make the filling.

Step 2: The filling

- Combine ½ cup of water with cornstarch and set aside.

- In a heavy saucepan, combine 1½ cups water and the cherry gelatin. Stir over a low heat, being sure not to let the mixture boil.

- Add the cornstarch mixture and brandy to the cherry mixture. Stir continuously until it thickens and becomes translucent.

- Remove from heat. Add all but 10 of the cherries. Stir and let cool.

- In a small bowl, beat the whipping cream to form soft peaks. Add vanilla and sweeten to taste.

- When the cherry mixture is cool, fold in ⅔ cup of the whipping cream.

Step 3: Assembling the cake

- Remove cakes from the pans by loosening sides with a thin knife and then turn over. Peel off the parchment paper or foil.

- Put one layer on a decorative serving plate.

- Using a spatula, spread cherry mixture over the top of cake.

- Then add a layer of whipping cream.

- Put second layer on top, add cherry mixture and decorate with the whipping cream and cherries

- Serve immediately or store in the refrigerator.

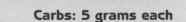

Yield: 10   Protein: 11 grams   Carbs: 5 grams each

Chocolate Coconut Coffee Cake

This sumptuous cake is easy to put together and has the added bonus of lots of fiber. It's a real crowd pleaser.

4 eggs
½ cup water
½ cup oil
1 heaping teaspoon unfla-
   vored gelatin
2 teaspoons baking powder
½ cup unsweetened cocoa
   powder

1 tablespoon cinnamon
¾ cup soy protein powder
½ cup flaxseed meal or psyllium
½ cup unsweetened coconut
1 cup sucralose
1½ cups chopped walnuts

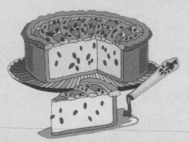

Preheat oven to 375°

- Put eggs, water, oil and gelatin in a large mixing bowl or food processor. Mix thoroughly.

- Add cinnamon, baking powder and cocoa; blend well.

- Mix in the protein powder, psyllium, sweetener and coconut.

- Put half of the walnuts on the bottom of a 9x13-inch baking pan. Add batter.

- Put remaining walnuts on top and press into batter with a fork.

- Bake for about 40 minutes.

- Cool thoroughly before serving.

- Butter is a delicious addition to this coffee cake.

Yield: 12   Protein: 7 grams   Carbs: 4.5 grams each

CRANBERRY WALNUT BREAD

Indulge yourself with this wonderful bread during the holidays when everyone else is complaining about unhealthy, sugary treats. It's moist, tangy and the perfect after-dinner indulgence.

2 eggs
Juice of two lemons
½ cup water
1 tablespoon grated lemon rind
1 tablespoon baking powder
2 cups soy protein powder

1 cup sucralose
2 teaspoons cinnamon
1 cup walnuts
1 cup whole cranberries

Preheat oven to 350°

- Put eggs, lemon juice, rind and water in a bowl or food processor and beat until completely combined.

- Sift together the baking powder, protein powder, sucralose and cinnamon. Add to the egg mixture and mix well.

- Stir in the walnuts and cranberries with a spoon.

- Spoon into a 9x5x3-inch greased pan and bake for about 55 minutes.

- When the bread has cooled, cut into thin slices.

Yield: 12   Protein: 10 grams   Carbs: 3 grams each

CHOCOLATE RASPBERRY TORTE

For a celebration or a "self-a-bration" this scrumptious torte will rise to the occasion. The taste is divine and it looks like a slice of chocolate heaven. Who says we can't have it all?

1 cup water
1 cup sucralose (or 1 tablespoon stevia)
1 bar unsweetened baking chocolate
1 stick of butter (4 ounces)
4 eggs
¼ cup brandy
3 tablespoons chocolate whey protein powder
1 tablespoon vanilla
1 cup raspberries
1 cup whipping cream
½ cup toasted pecans

Preheat oven to 350°

- In a medium saucepan, over a low flame, heat the water, sweetener and chocolate.

- Remove from heat when chocolate is melted and add butter.

- Put eggs and brandy in a large bowl or food processor and thoroughly mix.

- Add the protein powder to the egg mixture and completely incorporate.

- Stir the vanilla into the egg mixture.

- Next, whisk the cooled chocolate mixture until it is completely combined.

- Using a whisk or food processor, add the chocolate (a little at a time) to the egg mixture.

- Mix until frothy.

- Pour into a 6-inch round, lightly buttered, ceramic baking dish.

- Put this dish into a larger baking pan which has an inch of water on the bottom.

- Bake 40 minutes (it will have a custard-like texture).

- Remove from oven and let cool.

- When ready to serve, decorate with a ring of raspberries. Serve with whipped cream and toasted pecans.

Yield: 6   Protein: 7.5 grams   Carbs: 5 grams each

Maple Walnut Cake

This dessert has a wonderful flavor and unique texture. Because it is crumbly, slice and serve directly from the pan when cooled.

3 eggs
¼ cup oil
¼ cup lecithin granules
2 teaspoons imitation
   maple flavoring
¾ cup sucralose or other
   sweetener

1 cup chopped walnuts
1 cup soy protein powder

Preheat oven to 375°

- In a food processor or mixing bowl, combine the eggs, oil, lecithin, maple flavoring and sucralose.

- Add the protein powder and process until it becomes thick, like cookie dough. Mix in chopped nuts.

- Spoon into a 9x9-inch non-stick pan. Flatten with a fork.

- Bake for 15 minutes.

- Remove from the oven and sprinkle with a dusting of sucralose. Turn off oven and bake for about 5 more minutes or until the top is golden brown.

Yield: 12   **Protein 10 grams**   **Carbs: 2 grams each**

Lemon Chiffon Cake

∽

This light, tangy cake is easier to make than angel food, and every bit as delicious and versatile. It's wonderful topped with whipped cream and berries.

6 egg whites at room temperature
1 cup sucralose
5 egg yolks
6 tablespoons fresh lemon juice

1 tablespoon grated lemon peel
1¼ cups soy protein powder
½ teaspoon salt

Preheat oven to 350°

- In a large bowl, using an electric mixer, beat eggs whites until foamy. Gradually add ½ cup of sweetener. Continue beating until mixture forms firm peaks when beater is lifted.

- Beat egg yolks and then gradually blend in remaining sweetener. Add juice and lemon peel and beat for about another minute.

- At low speed, blend in protein powder and salt. Use a rubber spatula to feed the mixture into the beaters.

- Use the spatula to gently fold egg whites into batter, using an under and over motion. Be careful not to break down the whites.

- Pour batter into a 10-inch tube pan that has not been oiled. Bake for about 30 minutes.

- Invert pan over the neck of a bottle and let cool for about 1 hour.

- Use a spatula to carefully loosen cake from sides of the pan.

- This cake is delicious plain, iced or served with berries.

Yield: 10   Protein: 14 grams   Carbs: 2.5 grams each

STRAWBERRY CHEESECAKE

With its burst of strawberries, this light, luscious cheesecake brings summer into one's soul. Since it requires no baking, it's perfect for warm weather.

16 ounces cream cheese
1 cup sucralose
1 cup whipping cream
4 egg whites
1 teaspoon vanilla extract
2 teaspoons unflavored gelatin
1 cup water
1 cup chopped toasted nuts

- Stir unflavored gelatin into ½ cup boiling water until dissolved. Add remaining water and let cool in refrigerator.

- Beat cream cheese with ½ cup sweetener until fluffy.

- Add cream and beat until smooth.

- In another bowl, beat egg whites until frothy. Gradually add remaining sweetener and vanilla while continually beating until just stiff enough to form peaks.

- Fold eggs into cheese mixture.

- When the gelatin mixture becomes syrupy, fold into cheese mixture.

- Spread nuts on the bottom of a 9-inch springform pan, add batter and chill for 2 hours.

Strawberry Topping

1 cup sliced unsweetened
   strawberries
1 small package of diet
   strawberry gelatin
1½ cups water

- Dissolve gelatin in 1 cup boiling water.

- Add ½ cup cold water and stir well.

- Add strawberries to mixture and pour over
  the top of the cake when ready to serve.

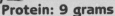

Yield: 10   Protein: 9 grams   Carbs: 5.5 grams each

Muffins
and Cupcakes

Chocolate Brandy Muffins

As an after-dinner coffee treat, these muffins can't be surpassed. The rich chocolate brandy flavor, spiked with chocolate chips and walnuts, gives the word muffin a whole new spin.

3 eggs
⅓ cup oil
¾ cup water
¼ cup brandy (or 1 teaspoon
   brandy extract and water)
1 vanilla bean or 2 teaspoons
   vanilla extract
⅓ cup lecithin

1 teaspoon baking soda
2 teaspoons baking powder
¾ cup psyllium
1 cup chocolate whey powder
¾ cup soy protein powder
1½ cups chopped walnuts
⅓ cup chocolate chips

Preheat oven to 375°

- Combine eggs, oil and water in a food processor or mixing bowl and beat until yellow and foamy.

- Add the brandy and vanilla. Mix well.

- Mix in the lecithin, soda, baking powder and psyllium, being sure that the powders are completely incorporated.

- Beat in the protein powders.

- Stir in the nuts and chips.

- Put batter into greased muffin tins.

- Bake for about 20 minutes, or until they are firm on top but still moist in the middle.

Yield: 12   Protein: 15 grams   Carbs: 4.5 grams each

LEMON POPPY SEED MUFFINS

If you are craving a snack that's delicious and healthy, this tart, tasty muffin is just the ticket. These gems are loaded with fiber ... a healthy boost for anyone's diet.

3 large lemons juiced
2 tablespoons finely grated
 lemon rind
4 eggs
5 tablespoons poppy seeds
2 tablespoons oil
¾ cup water

2 tablespoons lecithin granules
1 cup sucralose or other sweetener to taste
1½ tablespoons baking powder
Pinch of salt
1⅓ cups soy protein powder
⅓ cup psyllium

Preheat oven to 375°

- Grate the yellow peel of the lemon.

- Juice lemons and place in a food processor or mixing bowl.

- Add the water, oil, lecithin granules, sweetener, lemon peel and eggs. Blend completely.

- Mix in the protein powder, baking powder, salt, poppy seeds and psyllium.

- Spoon into non-stick muffin pans and bake for 20 minutes.

- Store in refrigerator.

Yield: 12   Protein: 9 grams   Carbs: 2.5 grams each

WALNUT STREUSEL MUFFINS

Everybody has their own take on muffins. For me, they were something only the skinny few could munch at one of those trendy coffee places. I felt like the fringe element, sitting at a table with just a magazine to accompany my Americana coffee.

Well, gone are the "days of deprivation" in the muffin-munching world. Here is the ultimate muffin.

These muffins are so "foo foo," you may still feel guilty eating them.

They keep wonderfully in a covered container. If you can keep out of the container, that is.

Muffin Ingredients

1 cup sucralose
½ cup soft butter or safflower oil
1 teaspoon vanilla extract
3 eggs
1½ cups protein powder
¼ cup psyllium husks
1 teaspoon baking soda
½ teaspoon salt
1 cup sour cream
½ cup nuts

Preheat oven to 350°

- In a large bowl or a food processor, combine the sweetener, butter and vanilla. Mix for one minute.

- Add eggs and combine until smooth.

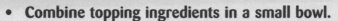

Topping

½ cup walnuts or pecans
¼ cup sucralose
1 teaspoon cinnamon
2 tablespoons soft butter (1 ounce)

- Combine topping ingredients in a small bowl.

- Mix until smooth, using a wooden spoon or a spatula.

- After batter is in pan, add tablespoons of the mixture to the top of each muffin.

- Put in the dry ingredients and mix well.

- Stir in the nuts and sour cream.

- Spoon batter into greased or non-stick muffin pans, leaving room to add a tablespoon of the topping.

- Add the topping and bake on the bottom rack of the oven for 15 minutes.

- They are delicious served warm from the oven.

Yield: 18   Protein: 8 grams   Carbs: 2.5 grams each

Orange Nut Muffins

Muffins are a wonderful way to start the day and this recipe is guaranteed to bring sunshine into the morning meal. These muffins are moist, zesty and the generous helping of nuts adds a delicious crunch to every bite.

1½ cups soy protein powder
½ cup psyllium or flaxseed meal
1 teaspoon cinnamon
1 teaspoon baking powder
¼ teaspoon salt
1 cup chopped walnuts
Grated peel of 1 orange

2 eggs
1 cup water
½ cup oil
1½ cups sucralose or other
    sweetener to taste
8 ounces cream cheese
1 tablespoon lemon juice

Preheat oven to 375°

- Sift together the first 5 ingredients.

- Mix in the nuts and orange zest.

- In another bowl, beat eggs and then stir in water, oil and <u>1 cup</u> of sweetener.

- Add egg mixture to dry ingredients and mix just until dry ingredients are moistened.

- Spoon into greased muffin cups, filling about two-thirds full.

- Bake about 12 to 15 minutes.

- While muffins are baking, combine cream cheese, lemon juice and ½ cup of sweetener in a blender or food processor.

- When muffins are cool, spread icing on top and store in refrigerator.

Yield: 12   Protein: 12 grams   Carbs: 3 grams each

ZESTY BLUEBERRY MUFFINS

These hearty muffins are the opposite of light and fluffy. They have a rich lemon flavor, 14 grams of protein and a hearty texture that is guaranteed to leave you "berry" satisfied.

Grated peel of 1 lemon
Juice of 2 lemons
½ cup water
⅓ cup oil
3 eggs
½ teaspoon salt
½ teaspoon baking soda

2 teaspoons baking powder
1 cup sucralose
1 cup soy protein powder
½ cup whey protein powder
½ cup psyllium
1 cup walnut pieces
½ cup blueberries

Preheat oven to 400°

- Grease muffin tins.
- Grate lemon peel and put in food processor or mixing bowl.
- Juice lemons and add to the peel.
- Mix in the water, eggs and oil.
- Add the salt, soda and baking powder and beat thoroughly.
- Incorporate the sweeteners.
- Add the psyllium and protein powders.
- When batter is thoroughly blended, mix in the walnuts by hand.
- Put heaping spoonfuls of the batter to the top of the tins.
- Then place a teaspoon of the blueberries into the center of each muffin.
- Bake for about 25 minutes, or until the muffins are firm and golden.

Yield: 12   Protein: 14 grams   Carbs: 3 grams each

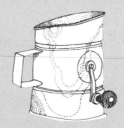

WITH AN ANGEL TOPPING
DEVIL'S FOOD CUPCAKES

The angels will be looking over your shoulder when you make these delicious moist cupcakes. They are made even more heavenly because the creamy topping is baked right into the cupcakes. Everyone loves these gems!

Cupcake Ingredients

1½ cups soy protein powder
⅓ cup psyllium powder
⅓ cup unsweetened cocoa powder
1¼ cups sucralose or other sweetener
½ teaspoon salt
1 teaspoon baking soda
1 cup water
½ cup vegetable oil
2½ teaspoons vanilla extract
2 teaspoons distilled white vinegar

Preheat oven to 350°

- Line 2 cupcake pans with paper liners or use non-stick pans.

- Sift together the protein powder, psyllium, cocoa, salt, baking soda and sucralose in a large bowl.

- Whisk together the water, oil, vanilla and vinegar in a small bowl.

- Pour the wet ingredients into dry ingredients and mix thoroughly.

- Fill each cupcake section a little more than half full.

Angel Topping Ingredients

12 ounces cream cheese
2 eggs
2½ teaspoons vanilla extract
1 cup chopped walnuts
¼ cup sucralose

(All ingredients should be at room temperature.)

- Make the topping by combining the cream cheese, eggs, vanilla and the remaining ¼ cup sucralose with a food processor or mixer. Blend completely for about 2 minutes and then add the nuts.

- Spoon a heaping tablespoon of icing on top of each cake.

- Bake for about 25 minutes on the lower rack of the oven. They are ready when a toothpick inserted into the center of the cake comes out clean and dry.

- Cool for a few minutes and then remove cupcakes from pan and cool to room temperature. Store in the refrigerator.

Yield: 18   Protein: 8 grams   Carbs: 4 grams each

Ice Cream

&
other creamy delights

Homemade Ice Cream
(Without an Ice Cream Maker)

My first successful ice cream venture was a big triumph. I felt like I had climbed Mount Everest without a Sherpa.

The challenge was making ice cream that is healthy, easy and would not require an ice cream maker.

Once again, the trusty food processor came to the rescue. There were several failures, that turned into shakes and other slurpy concoctions, but one day it all came together.

Some recipes use whole milk yogurt to replace a portion of the cream. The few extra carbs are worth the many health benefits. Unflavored gelatin is another vital ingredient for binding and additional protein.

Of course, adding nuts of your choice is always an option. Try pecans, almonds or walnuts.

So we can quit screaming for ice cream and celebrate this accomplishment. Hooray!

Fresh Strawberry Ice Cream

This wonderful frozen dessert is fresh, creamy and unsurpassed in low-carb scrumptiousness. And to make it even better, it's loaded with health boosters like yogurt, gelatin and vitamin C.

2 cups fresh, hulled strawberries
¾ cup sucralose
3 tablespoons vanilla whey
   protein powder

Juice of 1 lemon or 1 teaspoon
   vitamin C powder
2 eggs
1 cup plain, whole milk yogurt
1 teaspoon plain gelatin
2 cups very cold heavy cream

- Put yogurt, eggs, lemon juice, 1 teaspoon of the gelatin and protein powder in a food processor and mix until smooth.

- Add sweetener and strawberries and process until strawberries are barely chopped.

- Put into a large container and place in freezer until slushy.

- While the mixture is freezing, thoroughly clean the processor bowl and blade. If you have room, put bowl in the freezer.

- When strawberry mixture is about the texture of sherbet, put the cream and 1 teaspoon of gelatin in the processor and carefully mix until it thickens and forms peaks.

- Add the strawberry mixture and carefully combine by hand.

- At this stage, you can serve as a soft ice cream or put back in freezer until it has the texture of regular ice cream.

Yield: 8 (½ cup)   Protein: 9 grams   Carbs: 5 grams

ICE CREAM SUPREME

This ice cream can be served in bare elegance or embellished with nuts, berries or "Hot Fudge Topping". It's easy to feel like royalty while slowly savoring this delectable dessert.

Although this recipe can be made with 4 cups of cream, I opted to use half yogurt because of the health benefits.

This recipe requires an ice cream freezer. I was delighted to learn how easy it is to use this timesaving device. We prepared ice cream from start to finish in about 30 minutes.

It is best to serve the ice cream directly from the ice cream maker. It becomes too hard when stored in the freezer.

2 cups whipping cream
2 cups whole milk yogurt
1 cup sucralose
Scraping from a vanilla bean or
   1 tablespoon vanilla extract
2 tablespoons vanilla whey
   protein powder

- Combine all ingredients in a food processor.
- Pour into ice cream maker canister.
- Follow manufacturer's directions for freezing.

Yield: 12 (½ cup)   Protein: 3.5 grams   Carbs: 4 grams

♥ Hot Fudge Topping ♥

There are dozens of uses for this chocolate fudge sauce. We love it on cream puffs, ice cream and it's double decadence on brownies. Serve it hot or cold. It thickens when chilled.

½ cup water
¼ cup butter (2 ounces)
1 square unsweetened
   baker's chocolate

¾ cup sucralose or other
   low-carb sweetener to taste
3 tablespoons chocolate whey
   protein powder

- Put water, butter and unsweetened chocolate square in a small pan and melt over a low flame. (Microwaving works well, too.)

- Remove from heat and stir in sweetener and protein powder.

- This topping is quite thick. For a thinner sauce add more water or cream.

Yield: 12 tbsp.   Protein: 3 grams   Carbs: 2 grams each

Frozen Brandy Bombay

Indulgent elegance is the only way to describe this after-dinner delight. We have adapted this recipe from a dessert served at the New York Waldorf Astoria.

¾ cup water
1 cup sucralose
8 egg yolks

⅓ cup brandy
1 cup heavy cream

- Heat water and sweetener in a small saucepan, stirring until sucralose is dissolved. Let boil for 5 minutes.

- Mix egg yolks in a large bowl with an electric mixer.

- Very gradually, beat the sweetened water into the egg yolks. (Don't add it too quickly or you will cook the egg yolks.)

- Continue to beat until thickened and cooled.

- Gradually fold in brandy.

- Whip the cream in a chilled bowl with chilled beaters. When cream has thickened, fold in half of the egg mixture. Carefully fold the whipped cream into the remaining egg yolk mixture.

- Put mixture into a covered container and freeze for 8 hours.

- Serve with espresso drinks.

Yield: 8 (½ cup)   Protein: 1 gram   Carbs: 2 grams

RASPBERRY FROST

This delectable dessert is the pinnacle of self-indulgence. Served in a frosty crystal dessert dish, it looks like a pink arctic cloud.

1 cup frozen or fresh raspberries (or other favorite berry)
2 cups water
1 small (0.3 ounce) package diet raspberry gelatin
2 tablespoons lemon juice
1 teaspoon finely grated orange rind
1 cup cold whipping cream

- Put 1 cup water in a small container and heat to boiling. Sprinkle gelatin over the water and stir completely. When gelatin is dissolved, stir in 1 cup of cold water.

- Puree the raspberries in a food processor.

- Stir gelatin mixture into raspberry puree, along with lemon juice and orange rind. Thoroughly combine.

- Mix in the cream.

- Put the cream mixture in a covered container and chill in the refrigerator. When the mixture is thickened, put in the food processor and whip until it's the texture of whipped cream.

- Spoon into individual dessert cups and refrigerate for at least an hour.

- A few berries and more whipped cream make an over-the-top presentation.

Yield: 6 (½ cup)   Protein: 1 gram   Carbs: 5 grams

FANTASTIC FROZEN FUDGIES

One of my favorite childhood treats was Fudgsicles-- cold, chocolate creaminess on a stick. These can be made in a plastic frozen pop maker or in small paper cups with wooden sticks.

2 cups warm water
1 tablespoon unsweetened gelatin
1¼ cups chocolate whey protein
    powder
1 tablespoon lecithin granules

1 teaspoon vanilla extract
¾ cup sucralose (most low-carb
    sweeteners work well)
2 teaspoons unsweetened cocoa
    powder (optional)

- Put water and gelatin in the large bowl of food processor and mix well.

- Add remaining ingredients and blend thoroughly. Taste mixture and, if a deeper chocolate flavor is desired, add cocoa.

- Put mixture into ice-pop maker (or cups) and freeze until solid.

Yield: 6   Protein: 10 grams   Carbs: 2 grams each

CHOCOLATE ALMOND PUDDING

This creamy treat indulges any chocolate craving with a guilt-free conscience. The almonds add a satisfying crunch and the orange zest enhances the sublime flavor.

2 cups warm water
1 tablespoon unsweetened gelatin
¼ cup unsweetened cocoa powder
1 cup vanilla whey protein powder

2 tablespoons lecithin
1 teaspoon vanilla extract
¾ cup sucralose (most low-carb sweeteners work well)
1 teaspoon orange zest (optional)
½ cup chopped almonds

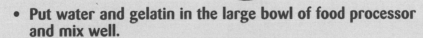

- Put water and gelatin in the large bowl of food processor and mix well.

- Add next 6 ingredients and blend thoroughly.

- Mix in chopped almonds and orange zest. Spoon into dessert cups.

- Put in refrigerator until thickened (at least 1 hour).

- Garnish with whipped cream and almonds.

Yield: 6 (½ cup)   **Protein: 8 grams**   **Carbs: 5 grams**

Chocolate Crème Brulee

We can have it all and crème brulee is no exception. The rich chocolatey flavor and scrumptious texture put this on the pinnacle of pleasure-- especially when embellished with strawberries and whipped cream.

2 cups whipping cream
2 ounces unsweetened
  baking chocolate
4 slightly beaten egg yolks
¾ cup sucralose

1 teaspoon vanilla extract
¼ teaspoon salt
Topping:
3 tablespoons sucralose
2 tablespoons brandy

Preheat oven to 325°

- Chop the chocolate and combine with whipping cream in a heavy pan or double boiler. Stir over a low flame until chocolate is melted.

- Remove from heat and let cool.

- Beat egg yolks, sucralose, vanilla and salt together in a large bowl.

- Using a whisk, slowly (and just a little at a time) add the cream mixture to the egg mixture.

- Put the batter in a small soufflé dish. Place the dish in a larger pan with 1 inch of boiling water in bottom of pan.

- Bake for 50 to 60 minutes or until knife inserted in the middle comes out clean.

- Remove brulee from oven and put on elevated rack to cool.

- To make the topping, put the 3 tablespoons of sucralose in a small heavy saucepan or skillet and heat over medium temperature. Shake occasionally until sweetener becomes golden brown. Mix in brandy.

  Drizzle the brandy mixture over the brulee.

- Let cool in refrigerator from 1 to 6 hours. It is a delightful finishing
- touch to any special meal.

Yield: 6   Protein: 1 gram   Carbs: 2 grams each

Bittersweet Chocolate Custard

Taking the first bite of this rich, creamy dessert is like entering the gates of chocolate heaven. This recipe takes a little time (and an ice cream maker) but it's well worth the effort.

1 cup half and half
1 cup sucralose
½ cup cocoa powder

4 egg yolks
2 cups whipping cream
1 teaspoon vanilla extract

- Place half and half, sucralose, cocoa and egg yolks in a food processor or blender and blend until smooth.

- Pour into a medium saucepan and stir over low heat. When bubbles start to form around edge of mixture, remove from heat.

- Put in refrigerator until chilled.

- Pour mixture into an ice cream maker and add whipping cream and vanilla.

- Follow manufacturer's directions for your ice cream freezer.

Yield: 8 (½ cup)   Protein: 1 gram   Carbs: 2.5 grams

ROYAL STRAWBERRIES AND CRÈME

This dessert is a royal spin on the traditional strawberries and cream. The cream is molded and surrounded with strawberries. A knockout treat for any dessert table, with a minimal carb boost.

1 cup cream
1½ teaspoons unflavored gelatin
½ cup sweetener

1 cup sour cream
1 teaspoon vanilla extract
1 pint strawberries

- In a small saucepan, combine the cream, gelatin and sweetener. Let sit for a few minutes while gelatin softens.

- Place mixture over moderate heat and stir until sweetener is dissolved.

- Put sour cream in small bowl of an electric mixer setup. Turn mixer to lowest speed and gradually add the hot cream and vanilla. Combine until smooth. Use a rubber spatula to scrape sides of bowl.

- Rinse a small 2½ cup gelatin mold (or shallow bowl) with cold water. Shake to remove water-- but don't dry.

- Put mixture in mold and refrigerate for at least 4 hours.

- Wash and slice strawberries into quarters, then sprinkle with a little sweetener. Refrigerate.

- When ready to serve, unmold crème by carefully running a small knife around the sides of the mold. Then dip bottom of the mold briefly into a shallow pan of hot water.

- Dry outside of mold and then place a serving dish over the top of mold and invert. If crème doesn't come out easily, dip it again.

- Serve slices of the crème with a generous amount of strawberries.

Yield: 6 (½ cup)   Protein: 2 grams   Carbs: 5 grams

(ECSTASY ON A PLATE)
CREAMY DREAMY PUFFS

It's hard to imagine eating cream puffs on a weight loss regime and (for me) it was even harder to imagine creating these mysterious mounds of marvel.

As it turns out, it's actually pretty easy. (Thanks to a food processor.)

Present a plate of these puffs at any gathering and enjoy the admiration in everyone's eyes. Best of all... zero carbs.

1 cup water
½ cup butter

1 heaping cup soy ~~protein~~ powder   flour?
3 eggs

11/04

Preheat oven to 400°

- Put butter and water in a quart sized pan over medium heat. When butter is melted, add soy powder and stir by hand until mixture forms a ball and doesn't stick to sides of pan.

- Let the mixture stand for about 5 minutes and then put in a food processor.

- Add the eggs (one at a time) through the tube as the processor is spinning.

- After the last egg is mixed in, turn off processor and scrape dough from the sides with a spatula.

- Drop about 2 tablespoons of the dough onto parchment paper covered or non-stick pans. Allow about 3 inches between each puff.

- Bake for about 40 minutes. Puffs should be lightly browned and sound hollow when tapped with your knuckles.

- Fill with whipped cream. Add fresh berries for a sumptuous presentation.

Yield: 8   Protein: 15 grams   Carbs: 0

Dough was *very* runny. Cooked in 1 large pool. Tore it into bits + made trifle.

Lemon whipped cream or sauce, would be heavenly!

CHEESECAKE SOUFFLÉ

If you like the flavor of cheesecake and the light-ness of a soufflé, this recipe is the answer to your dessert dreams. This method of making a soufflé is easier than most, and the results are spectacular.

11/04 good flavor

6 eggs (room temperature)
5 tablespoons sucralose
1 lemon
1 teaspoon vanilla extract
6 ounces cream cheese
2 teaspoons lemon zest
¼ tsp lemon extract

Preheat oven to 400°

- Prepare a 6 to 8 cup soufflé mold (or a small round baking dish) by spreading butter evenly around the insides and rim of the container. Sprinkle with 1 tablespoon of the sucralose and refrigerate mold.

- Separate the eggs, putting the whites into a medium-sized bowl and yolks in a larger bowl.

- Beat the yolks and 2 tablespoons of the sweetener until thickened.

- Put a few drops of lemon juice and vanilla into the egg whites and beat until foamy. Gradually add the remaining sweetener and beat until firm and glossy. (Do not over beat.)

- Place the lemon zest into the egg yolk mixture along with ~~the remaining sweetener and~~ cream cheese. Beat until creamy.

- Carefully fold egg whites into yolk mixture.

- Gently spoon the mixture into the prepared mold.

- Bake for about 12 *minutes. Soufflé should be puffy and browned on top.

- Serve immediately, garnished with a few raspberries.

small portions

Yield: 6   Protein: 10 grams   Carbs: 2 grams each

* Took @ 20 min in brown dish. Next time use wider bowl.

The Wonderful World of
Whipped Cream

Whipping Cream-- that magical ingredient that creates mounds of pristine pleasure and takes any simple dessert to the top of the elegance scale.

We don't consider whipped cream that chemical stuff in a can-- but it can be a hassle to stop in the middle of an elaborate party and make the real stuff. There is a way to make the topping before the party. The "Really Cool Whipped Topping" can be refrigerated for up to 3 days.

Probably the most important factor in making perfect whipped cream is to be certain the utensils are thoroughly cleaned and dried. It is also essential that the cream is very cold. I sometimes put the cream carton in the freezer for 30 minutes before starting the whipping procedure.

Flavored whipped cream is another subtle delight that will have guests doing a double taste.

This versatile topping makes a sublime base for cake decorating, especially when embellished with fresh flowers. Check out the "Fresh Flower Cake Decor" section. These ideas are certain to provide a sweet relief from sugary icings.

Pure Pleasure Whipped Cream

This is simple pleasure taken to the extreme. This recipe can easily be doubled or tripled for any size dessert project.

1 cup ice cold whipping cream
1 teaspoon vanilla extract
Low-carb sweetener to taste
(about ¼ cup sucralose)

- This whipping cream can be made in a blender or with an electric mixer. It is important that the utensils are clean, dry and chilled.

- At least a half hour before whipping the topping, put the cream in a medium sized mixing bowl (or blender) and chill along with the beaters. This assures success every time.

- When ready to serve, whip cream until it begins to hold a shape.

- Add vanilla and sweetener and beat thoroughly.

- Spread, spoon or use a pastry bag to complete any dessert project.

Yield: 10 tbsp.   Protein: 0   Carbs: 1 gram each

Really Cool Whipped Topping

This wonderful cream has the staying power of ready-made toppings, but none of the preservatives and chemicals.

It tastes deliciously fresh and can be refrigerated for up to 3 days.

11/04 ☺ Gelatin mixture "clotted" as soon as it hit the cold cream, so topping had tiny

- 1 teaspoon unflavored gelatin
- 1 tablespoon warm water
- 1 tablespoon vanilla extract
- 1 cup heavy cream
- ¼ cup sucralose (or any low-carb sweetener)

brown blobs throughout.

- Put utensils and whipping cream in the refrigerator or freezer for at least 30 minutes before preparing the topping.

- Place gelatin, water and vanilla in a cup and stir until gelatin is dissolved.

- Add 1 tablespoon of the cream to the gelatin mixture and put aside.

- Add remaining cream to bowl and whip until mixture starts to thicken.

- Add sweetener and gelatin mixture and beat until it holds a firm shape.

- Refrigerate in an airtight container for up to 3 days.

Yield: 10 tbsp.   Protein: 0   Carbs: 1 gram each

MOCHA TOPPING

An incredible topping for all chocolate creations, this mocha cream is simple, subtle and satisfying. We have served it on brownies and enjoyed a multitude of mmms.

1 cup whipping cream
1 tablespoon instant coffee granules
¼ cup sucralose (any low-carb sweetener
    works well)

- Start with a thoroughly clean and dry blender or mixing bowl setup. If time allows refrigerate blender or beaters for at least 30 minutes.

- Place very cold whipping cream in the chilled bowl and whip the cream until it starts to thicken. Add remaining ingredients and beat until the consistency of a thick sauce.

- This can be spooned or poured on any dessert.

- It is a delicious addition to after-dinner coffee.

Yield: 10 tbsp. Protein: 0 Carbs: 1 gram each

CHOCOLATE WHIPPED CREAM

This chocolate creamy delight takes minutes to make but creates a sublime topping or filling for a myriad of desserts. The whey protein powder gives an extra health boost and eliminates the need for a sweetener.

Just give your most subtle Mona Lisa smile when people ask how you can be losing so much weight and still have indulgences like this.

1 cup whipping cream
2 tablespoons chocolate whey
    protein powder
1 teaspoon vanilla

- Make sure blender or mixer is clean and dry. If time allows, refrigerate beaters or blender for at least 30 minutes.

- When ready to create the topping, place all ingredients in a bowl or blender and whip until the cream is thickened and holds a shape.

- This tastes divine on ice cream, cakes or brownies.

- The whipped cream can be made ahead of time and refrigerated for up to 2 days. Be sure to store in a sealed glass container.

Yield: 10 tbsp.   Protein: 2 grams   Carbs: 1 gram each

ORANGE BRANDY CREAM

This cream is a decadently delicious treat that can be used as a topping, filling or icing on cakes and brownies. The hearty splash of brandy makes this strictly an adult treat

11/04 Great flavor.

2 teaspoons unflavored gelatin = 1 pkg.
2 tablespoons water
1¼ cups whipping cream
½ cup sucralose

⅓ cup brandy, rum, whiskey (or flavored extract)
1 tablespoon orange zest
¼ tsp. orange extract

- Sprinkle the gelatin over the water in a small heat-proof cup and let stand for about 5 minutes.

- Place cup in a small saucepan containing 1 inch of hot water.

- Stir gelatin over moderate heat until dissolved.

- Remove cup from heat and put in freezer* for about 15 minutes.

- In a chilled bowl with chilled beaters, whip the cream, sweetener and ¼ cup brandy until thickened.

- Stir a heaping tablespoon of the cream into the chilled gelatin and stir well. Add remaining brandy to cream mixture.

- Immediately add the gelatin to the bowl of cream and beat until it holds a definite shape.

- Stir in the orange zest.

- This mixture should be refrigerated until ready to serve.

*Turned to rubber; had to be microwaved. Try 5-8 min or place in larger bowl of ice water.

Yield: 15 tbsp.   Protein: 0   Carbs: 1 gram each

We layered this with "cream puff" pieces for a great Trifle.

Fresh Flowers & Cream Décor

The beauty of a dessert topped with mounds of whipped cream and adorned with fresh flowers is unsurpassable. The variety of colors and flowers makes the possibilities of this decorating method too numerous to ponder.

It is such an enjoyable and simple procedure. Your friends will think you hired a party planner.

irst step in creating a beautifully decorated cake is deciding on a color palate. This color scheme can be implemented with a variety of colored creams and fresh flowers in matching or contrasting colors. The results can be a virtual garden of beauty.

I prefer to decorate with flat flowers like small rose buds, nasturtiums, or pansies.

The choices are endless, but <u>do not use daisies, sunflowers, marigolds or oleander</u>. <u>The first three taste and smell horrific and the oleander is poisonous</u>.

Big flowers (like tulips) do not hold up well. However, orchids can be the one exception. They look magnificent and last through an entire evening.

Once you have made you choices, rinse the flowers very carefully in cool water and let dry on a few layers of paper towels. Refrigerate until ready to use.

Frost your cake with the "Really Cool Whipped Topping" or another icing of your choice. When you are ready to bring out the cake, arrange the flowers in a magnificent display.

Try a heart arrangement of red rosebuds on white whipped cream for Valentine's Day. Using beautiful paper doilies to cover the cake dish is another elegant touch.

We did a beautiful birthday cake in a pink and white motif. After covering the cake with half the whipped cream topping, we mixed cranberry juice concentrate and a little vanilla whey protein powder into the remaining cream. We then put the pink cream in a pastry bag and wrote the birthday letters. We finished the creation with pink stars and baby rose buds.

Another idea for coloring or flavoring the icing is to mix strawberry or chocolate protein powder into the whipped cream. You can also use food coloring.

For longer lasting blossoms, we have dipped the fresh flowers in hot wax before decorating the cake. They keep for months and can be reused. Of course, remove the flowers before serving.

Let your imagination blossom!

Pies

BROWNIE FUDGE PIE

∽

Each delicious bite of this rich fudgey pie is a culinary delight.   For sheer indulgence, top this with dollops of whipping cream.

Doug:
10/04 Dry;
aftertaste
David — fix it again

1 cup sucralose
2 eggs
½ cup soft butter
½ cup soy protein powder
3 tablespoons cocoa

1 teaspoon vanilla extract
2 teaspoons instant coffee crystals
⅔ cup chopped walnuts
Whipped cream

Preheat oven to 325°

- In a mixing bowl or food processor, put all the ingredients except nuts and whipped cream. Beat for several minutes.

- Stir in nuts.

- Pour into greased 9-inch pie pan. *or smaller*

- Bake for 30 minutes. *or less*

- Remove from oven and cool. Pie will settle while cooling.

- Whip the cream and add a generous dollop to each serving.

Yield: 8   Protein: 8 grams   Carbs: 4 grams each

CREAM CHEESE PIE

This pie is a double dip of delight for those who love rich and creamy desserts. This dessert will take star billing on any

1 cup chopped walnuts
12 ounces cream cheese
   at room temperature
1 teaspoon vanilla extract
1½ cups sucralose

3 tablespoons whey
   protein powder
2 eggs
½ cup heavy cream
2 cups sour cream

Preheat oven to 350°

- *Adjust oven rack to lowest setting before preheating.*
- *In a small bowl, using an electric mixer at low speed, beat cream cheese until smooth. Add vanilla and 1 cup of the sweetener.*
- *Increase mixer speed to medium and beat in eggs, one at a time.*
- *Add protein powder. Use a rubber spatula to help push mixture into beaters.*
- *Pour in the heavy cream and beat until just smooth.*
- *Put walnuts into 9-inch pie pan and top with cream mixture.*
- *Bake for 25 minutes and then remove from oven. Turn oven down to 300°.*
- *Allow oven to cool for 20 minutes.*
- *While oven is cooling, combine sour cream and remaining sweetener.*
- *Carefully spread sour cream mixture on top of the pie.*
- *Return to the 300° oven for only 5 minutes.*
- *Remove from oven and let cool before refrigerating. Chill for several hours.*

Yield: 8   Protein: 10 grams   Carbs: 5.5 grams each

A Slice of Heaven
Fresh Strawberry Pie

We can now celebrate the fact that fruit pies are no longer taboo in low-carb cuisine. This luscious pie tastes so fresh, it brings to mind the joys of summer. It's easy to make and makes a glorious presentation on any dessert table.

3 cups fresh strawberries
1 small package diet strawberry
   gelatin
2 cups water
½ cup sour cream
1 teaspoon vanilla extract
1 cup whipping cream

- **Prepare and bake the crust (see piecrust recipes).**

- **Clean strawberries and thinly slice. Store in a bowl.**

- **Boil one cup water. Pour water into a bowl and add the gelatin. Stir well, until the crystals are dissolved. Add 1 cup of cold water to the gelatin.**

- **When piecrust has cooled, put the strawberries in the shell.**

- Add ½ cup sour cream and vanilla to the gelatin mixture and beat thoroughly. Pour over the strawberries. Be careful to cover the entire top of the pie.

- Refrigerate for about 4 hours.

- When ready to serve, whip the cream and add a generous portion to each slice.

Almond Crumble Piecrust

1 cup almonds
⅓ cup cooking oil
1 egg
⅓ cup sucralose
½ cup vanilla whey protein powder
⅓ cup soy protein powder

- Put almonds and oil in a food processor and coarsely chop.

- Add egg and sucralose; mix well.

- Combine the protein powders with the mixture and process until the powders are absorbed.

- Spoon mixture into a 9-inch pie tin and use fingers, or a fork, to press into the bottom of the pan.

- Bake in the oven for about 10 minutes, or until crust is golden brown.

Yield: 8   Protein: 5 grams   Carbs: 5 grams each

LUSCIOUS LEMONY PIE

Tangy, tantalizing and absolutely irresistible, this pie favors the tarter side of tastes. It's easy to make but requires a few hours of refrigeration.

1½ cups chopped pecans
3 large eggs
½ cup fresh lemon juice
  (about three lemons)

1 tablespoon plain gelatin
⅓ cup soy protein powder
¾ cup sucralose
⅔ cup heavy cream

Preheat oven to 325°

- Spread pecans in 9-inch pie tin.

- Put remainder of ingredients in bowl with electric mixer. Mix until well combined and frothy.

- Place the pan with the pecans on the middle rack of oven. Carefully spoon in lemon filling.

- Bake for 20 minutes or until the mixture shimmers and seems slightly under cooked. Turn off heat and let pie stay in the oven for about 20 minutes.

- Chill in refrigerator for several hours before serving.

Yield: 8   Protein: 5 grams   Carbs: 5 grams each

MOCHA CHIFFON PIE

This is the ultimate after-dinner indulgence. The wonderful consortium of chocolate, brandy and coffee creates a dessert to remember.

1 tablespoon unflavored gelatin = 1½ pkgs
¾ cup strong coffee
2 tablespoons unsweetened cocoa
1 cup sucralose
3 tablespoons whey protein powder
4 eggs
1 teaspoon vanilla

1 tablespoon brandy
1 cup toasted walnuts or pecans, chopped.
1 cup whipping cream (for topping)

11/07 good

Preheat oven to 350°

- Mix gelatin and hot coffee in a medium-sized bowl. — *double boiler top.*

- Add cocoa and only ½ cup of the sweetener and mix well.

- Beat 4 egg yolks into chocolate mixture.

- Put the mixture in a double boiler and stir over low heat until it thickens. *3-4 min.*

- Refrigerate until it becomes the consistency of pudding.

- Remove from refrigerator and beat with an electric mixer until it becomes light and fluffy.

- Beat in protein powder, vanilla and brandy.

- Whip egg whites until stiff (but not dry) and slowly add remaining sweetener. *½ c.*

- Fold egg whites into chocolate mixture.

- Put toasted nuts on bottom of 9-inch pie pan and add filling.

- Chill in refrigerator.

- Serve with whipped cream.

Yield: 8   Protein: 7 grams   Carbs: 4.5 grams each

JAMAICAN RUM PIE

Rum and chocolate are the star players in this wonderful pie that is sure to be the hit of any occasion. One taste will take your taste buds on a mini Caribbean cruise.

Step 1: Walnut Crust

1½ cups walnuts
2 tablespoons sucralose
1 teaspoon cinnamon
1 tablespoon vanilla whey powder

Preheat oven to 375°

- *Coarsely chop nuts in food processor.*
- *Place on cookie sheet and toast in oven for about 10 minutes.*
- *Stir occasionally to be certain nuts are evenly browned.*
- *Remove from oven and place in a 9-inch pie tin.*
- *Add remaining ingredient to the hot nuts and stir well.*
- *Let cool while preparing the filling.*

Step 2: The Filling

    1 tablespoon unflavored gelatin
    ¼ cup water
    3 egg yolks
    1 cup sucralose
    ¼ cup light rum or 1 teaspoon rum
       extract with ¼ cup water
    1 cup heavy cream
    ½ square unsweetened chocolate or
       chilled, low-carb chocolate bar

- *Sprinkle gelatin over hot water and mix thoroughly.*
- *Beat egg yolks in a medium-sized bowl until thick and fluffy.*
- *Gradually add sweetener, mixing well after each addition.*
- *Add rum and gelatin mixture to egg yolks and beat thoroughly.*
- *In a chilled bowl, whip cream and carefully fold into egg mixture.*
- *Pour into cooled nut mixture.*
- *Refrigerate for 2 to 3 hours.*
- *Shave the chocolate over the pie when ready to serve.*

Yield: 8   **Protein: 9 grams**   **Carbs: 5 grams each**

Coconut Almond Cookie Crust

This crust is so delicious that the filling is almost secondary. It's so easy, and doesn't even require a rolling pin. Top it with your favorite filling or try strawberries, vanilla ice cream and our low-carb chocolate sauce.

½ cup raw almonds
¼ cup oil
2 eggs
Juice of one lemon
1 cup soy protein powder
2 tablespoons unsweetened
   coconut strands
1 cup sucralose or other low-
   carb sweetener to taste

Preheat oven to 375°

- **Put almonds in a food processor and use short bursts until nuts are roughly chopped.**

- **Remove from bowl.**

- **Put eggs and lemon juice in the processor and combine until frothy.**

- **Add remaining ingredients and mix well.**

- **Put the mixture in a 9-inch round pie tin and then add the nuts. Use a fork to press dough into bottom of the pan.**

- **Bake in oven until golden brown, about 12 minutes.**

Yield: 8   Protein: 10 grams   Carbs: 5 grams each

CHOCOLATE COOKIE CRUST

This crust is a luxurious foundation for any of the pie recipes. A food processor makes this pastry a simple pleasure.

½ cup soft butter
½ cup sucralose
½ teaspoon salt
2 teaspoons vanilla extract
2 tablespoons cold water

2 tablespoons unsweetened cocoa powder
1 cup soy protein powder

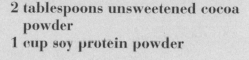

- Place butter, sweetener, salt and vanilla in the bowl of a food processor equipped with the metal blade. Process until creamy. Add water.

- Add cocoa and mix for 1 minute.

- Put in the protein powder and blend well.

- Remove dough from processor and wrap in plastic. Refrigerate for at least 1 hour.

- Half an hour before removing dough from refrigerator, preheat oven to 350°.

- Place chilled dough in a 9-inch round pie pan and press the dough over the bottom and sides of the pan.

- Bake in the pre-heated oven for about 12 minutes. Let cool for about ½ hour before adding your favorite pie filling.

Yield: 8   Protein: 12 grams   Carbs: 4 grams each

Candies

ALMOST SINFUL STRAWBERRIES

Chocolate dipped strawberries look exquisite and taste so divine, you might feel a tinge of guilt reaching for one of these natural favorites. Leave guilt behind-- the carb count is so low, you can indulge for around 3 carbs a berry. Another advantage of this fabulous treat is that it takes only 10 minutes from plan to platter.

½ bar of unsweetened baking chocolate
2 tablespoons butter
1 teaspoon vanilla
½ cup sucralose
10 medium-sized fresh strawberries

- Place chocolate and butter in a small, ceramic bowl and cover with a plate.

- Microwave on high for about one minute. Mixture should be soft, but not liquid.

- Add vanilla and sucralose; mix completely.

- Dip one side of the strawberry into chocolate mixture and place on a lightly buttered platter.

- Put in the freezer or refrigerator for a few minutes to harden the chocolate.

- Serve with dark, strong coffee or champagne.

Yield: 10   Protein: 1 gram   Carbs: about 3 grams each

MACADAMIA FUDGE

Take your taste buds on an exotic adventure with this delicious candy. The combination of chocolate and macadamia nuts is bound to take you to the land of "Too Good to Be True."

A big bonus with this easy recipe is that it requires no cooking and can be made in minutes. The second that chocolate craving crashes on the scene, whip up a batch of fudge, roll into balls and begin experiencing sweet satisfaction in less than ten minutes.

You can vary the taste of this candy by using liqueurs instead of extracts.

5 tablespoons chocolate whey protein powder
2 tablespoons unsweetened cocoa powder
⅓ cup soft butter
1 tablespoon vanilla or chocolate extract
2 tablespoons canola or mild tasting oil
¾ cup sucralose (or sweeten to taste)
¾ cup chopped macadamias (or other nuts)

11/04 very easy good; moist some aftertaste— try liqueurs.

- **Combine first 6 ingredients in a food processor until <u>well</u> mixed. Add the nuts and mix by hand.**

- **Put fudge on a buttered plate and flatten with the bottom of a glass until about ¼-inch thick. (You can also form balls by hand.)**

- **Put in freezer for about 10 minutes and then cut into squares. Serve on a lovely plate or in candy cups for an elegant touch.**

Yield: 12   Protein: 5 grams   Carbs: 2.5 gram each

Keep refrigerated

CHOCOLATE ALMOND CLUSTERS

These decadent candies are so easy to make that I have prepared and served them in 15 minutes. I usually make this delicacy when company is coming for dinner. They make a big splash as an after-dinner treat when served with strong coffee.

1 unsweetened bar of baking chocolate
2 tablespoons butter
1 cup sucralose
1 teaspoon vanilla extract
1 cup whole roasted almonds

- Place chocolate and butter in a small glass bowl and microwave for about one minute. Check mixture to be sure it is melted.

- When softened, add the sweetener and vanilla. Stir well. *Stir in nuts.*

- Put teaspoons of the mixture into paper candy cups or onto a buttered platter.

- Put in refrigerator or freezer until chocolate hardens.

Yield: 20   Protein: 1 gram   Carbs: 2.5 grams each

BRANDY BALLS

This exotic candy can make any day feel like a holiday. It's simple to make, and a healthy treat never had such a heady taste. So why not celebrate?

10/04 good, easy

½ cup strong coffee
2 tablespoons unflavored brandy
  or bourbon
1 tablespoon light cooking oil
Scraping of a vanilla bean
  (or 1 teaspoon of vanilla extract)

¾ cup chocolate or vanilla
  whey protein powder *
½ cup chopped walnuts
Sucralose to taste – 6 Tblsp

- Scrape the seeds out of the vanilla bean and soak them in brandy for 10 minutes.

- Combine coffee, oil and brandy-vanilla mixture in a medium-sized bowl or food processor.

- Mix in protein powder and add sucralose to taste.

- Add chopped nuts and roll heaping teaspoons of the mixture into balls.

- Refrigerate in a covered bowl for at least half an hour. *Better next day*

* Used milk & egg protein + 1 Tblsp. cocoa powder.

Yield: 16   Protein: 5 grams   Carbs: 2 grams each

COCONUT BON BONS

This delectable treat is rich and creamy on the inside with a thin layer of chocolate and coconut topping. This fabulous indulgence makes you want to sit on a chaise lounge and munch your guilt-free bon bons.

½ cup soft butter
2 tablespoons safflower oil
½ cup sucralose
½ cup coconut

4 tablespoons vanilla whey protein powder
⅓ cup semi-sweet chocolate chips

- Combine butter, oil, and sweetener in a food processor.
- Add only half of the coconut and all of the whey powder. Mix well.
- Taking heaping teaspoons of the mixture, form into balls and put on a plate.
- Refrigerate the balls for 15 minutes.
- Just before serving the bon bons, microwave chocolate chips with a tablespoon of butter for about 1 minute. Be careful to just soften, not liquefy.
- Dip top of each candy into chocolate and then into the remaining coconut.
- They can be returned to refrigerator for a few minutes to harden the chocolate.

Yield: 16   Protein: 4 grams   Carbs: 2 grams each

Spicy Candied Walnuts

These walnuts are a taste of forgotten heaven for the longtime carb watcher. They are a light, crunchy, cinnamon-spiced delight. So change your life from "Whoa" to "Go!!"

1 large egg white
1 teaspoon salt
1 teaspoon cinnamon
½ cup sucralose
1 cup raw walnuts

Preheat oven to 375°

- In a small bowl, whip egg white with an electric beater until it starts to thicken and turn white.

- Stir in salt, cinnamon and sucralose.

- Add walnuts to the mixture and stir until thoroughly coated.

- Put walnuts, one at a time, on a non-stick cookie sheet and bake in oven for about 10 minutes.

- Turn walnuts over and let bake for about another 5 minutes. Nuts should be dry, browned and crispy.

Yield: 25 walnut halves   Protein: 1 gram   Carbs: 1 gram each

GALLOPING GOURMET
VANILLA CHIPPIES

Saddle up your sweet tooth for a taste adventure on the satisfaction express. When you crave a sweetie with just an occasional crunch of chocolate, try these delicious candies. They can go from bowl to "bowl you over" in less than 10 minutes.

½ cup soft butter
2 tablespoons safflower or other mild tasting oil
½ cup sucralose (any low-carb sweetener can be used)
1 tablespoon vanilla extract or scraping of 1 whole vanilla bean

4 tablespoons vanilla whey protein powder
¼ cup semi-sweet chocolate chips
½ cup chopped pecans

- Put butter, sucralose and oil *+ vanilla* in a food processor and mix well.

- Add protein powder, chips and pecans. Stir by hand until powder is thoroughly incorporated.

- Form teaspoonfuls of the mixture into balls and place on a plate or in paper candy cups.

- Candy can be served immediately or refrigerated for a firmer texture.

Yield: 20   Protein: 4 grams   Carbs: 1.5 grams each

Shakes & Drinks

No matter how tight your time schedule, it's easy to create a delicious, quick meal with a blender and a few key ingredients.

Shakes are not only nourishing but can give a real boost when your willpower is shaky. Just blend it, pour it in a sports cup and be off and running.

Shakes are especially handy before exercising, when a big meal might make you feel too lethargic to put on those tennies and go.

Most low-carb shakes taste flat and boring, but these recipes are creamy, delicious and spiked with health giving nutrients.

So shake it up, you winner you!

MOCHA  KICKER

Here's the shake that will get you in your sweats and out the door during the most stubborn case of "I'm so tired... I want to stay home and veg."

So get to the blender, give yourself a hug and create this easy picker-upper!

1¼ cups cold, strong coffee
1 tablespoon flaxseeds (optional)
2 tablespoons cream (optional)
2 tablespoons vanilla or chocolate whey protein powder
Sweetener to taste
Crushed ice

- Put liquid and flaxseeds in a blender and process on high speed for about a minute.
- Add remaining ingredients (except the ice) and process thoroughly.
- Add ice and blend until frothy.

Yield: 1   Protein: 20 grams   Carbs: 2 grams each

VANILLA MOCHA FRAPPE

Thick, creamy and "jet-some" describes this gourmet coffee drink. Who needs those carb-laden, coffee store drinks?

1 cup cold strong coffee
1 teaspoon unflavored gelatin
1 teaspoon vanilla
2 tablespoons whey protein powder
¼ cup cream
Crushed ice
Zero-carb sweetener to taste

- Put coffee, vanilla and gelatin in blender and process for a few minutes.

- Add protein powder and mix well.

- Sweeten to taste.

- Add cream and ice cubes. Process until ice is dissolved. Turn blender on and off to prevent motor burn out.

Yield: 1   Protein: 22 grams   Carbs: 2 grams each

"You Deserve a Break"
Strawberry Shake

This strawberry shake is quick, easy and loaded with protein. A few frozen strawberries give this drink lots of flavor and pizzazz.

1¼ cups water
1 tablespoon flaxseeds (optional)
1 heaping teaspoon unflavored gelatin
1 tablespoon lecithin granules
2 tablespoons strawberry (or vanilla)
   whey protein powder
4 frozen strawberries

- In a blender, combine flaxseeds and water for about a minute on high speed.
- Add dry ingredients and process until smooth.
- Add frozen berries and blend thoroughly.

Yield: 1   Protein: 22 grams   Carbs: 4 grams each

Peachy & Creamy

Since most fruits are loaded with carbohydrates, a peach shake would appear to be out of the low-carb picture. It was a joy to discover that a delicious fruity shake can be created with a natural flavored drink mix.

1¼ cups water
1 tablespoon flaxseeds (optional)
1 teaspoon unflavored gelatin
2 tablespoons vanilla whey protein powder
1 heaping teaspoon low-carb, peach flavored drink mix (I prefer Crystal Light Peach/Raspberry.)
¼ teaspoon Vitamin C crystals (optional)
Sweetener (optional)
Crushed ice

- Put water and flaxseeds in a blender and process until seeds are pulverized.

- Add remaining ingredients (except ice) and blend until smooth.

- Add ice and process until creamy.

Yield: 1   Protein: 22 grams   Carbs: 1 gram each

CREAMY CHOCOLATE SHAKE

Thick, creamy shakes might seem taboo for the lactose intolerant, but this delicious shake breaks down the culinary barriers.

This recipe covers many nutritional bases besides providing lots of protein. Gelatin is great for nails, hair and joints and lecithin is important for the heart and brain.

1¼ cups water
2 tablespoons chocolate whey
    protein powder
1 tablespoon lecithin granules
2 teaspoons unflavored gelatin
1 teaspoon vanilla
Sweetener to taste
Crushed ice

- Put all ingredients (except ice) in a blender.
- Blend until frothy.
- Add ice cubes and process until smooth.

Yield: 1   Protein: 22 grams   Carbs: 4 grams each

FRUITY ICE TEA

Why not make ice tea a healthy drink? Use green tea (noted for its health giving properties) and real lemon for flavor. Keep a pitcher of this refreshing drink in the refrigerator.

4 cups boiling water
4 green tea bags
Juice of one lemon
Low-carb sweetener (to taste)

- Put the tea bags and boiling water in a quart container. Let tea steep for about 2 minutes.

- Remove tea bags and cool tea in the refrigerator.

- Add lemon juice after the tea has cooled, so the vitamin C is not destroyed.

- Sweeten to taste and serve in a tall glass with ice.

Yield: 4   Protein: 0   Carbs: 1 gram each

"Made in the Shade" Lemonade

Nothing quenches a thirst like a big frosty glass of fresh lemonade. It tastes delicious and is a superior internal body cleanser.

1 cup water
½ lemon
Zero-carb sweetener to taste
Ice cubes

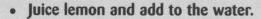

- Juice lemon and add to the water.
- Sweeten to taste and serve with ice cubes.
- A sprig of mint is a delightful touch.

Yield: 1   Protein: 0   Carbs: 2 grams

Root Beer Supreme

If you love root beer but avoid it because of aluminum cans and chemicals, then this root beer recipe is a real find. We don't even have to search in the woods for sacred roots and herbs, a root beer concentrate can be found in specialty stores.

Children love this delicious treat, especially with a little whipping cream. It makes it taste like a root beer float.

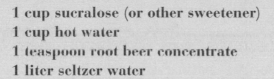

1 cup sucralose (or other sweetener)
1 cup hot water
1 teaspoon root beer concentrate
1 liter seltzer water

- Pour hot water into a large glass container and add sweetener. Stir until all crystals are dissolved.

- Add the root beer concentrate and cool in the refrigerator.

- Now would be a good time to frost some root beer mugs. To frost, just rinse mugs in spring water and put in the freezer.

- When ready to serve, add seltzer water to the concentrate and pour into chilled mugs.

Yield: 6 cups   Protein: 0   Carbs: 3 grams each

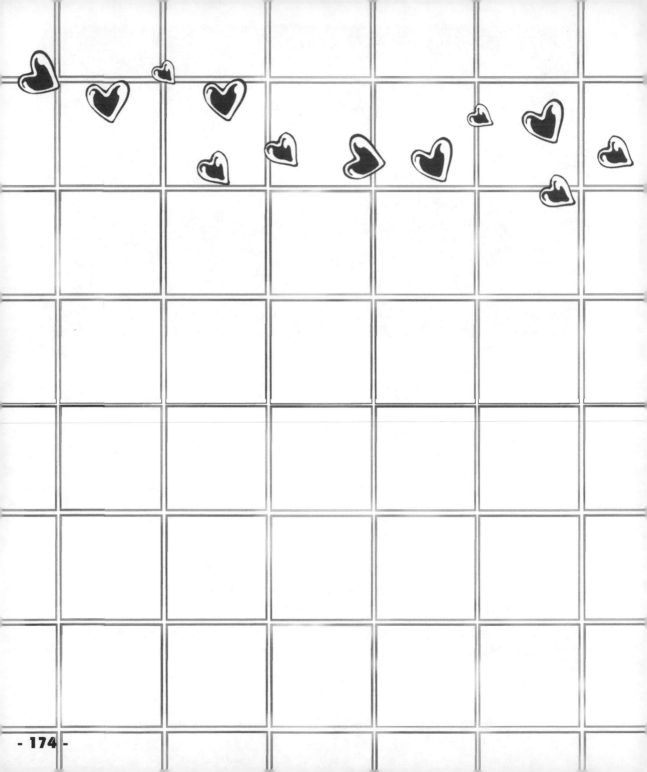

THE ART OF SELF-INDULGENCE

Step into Your Dream

Being able to eat the foods we love, while still slimming down to the body of our dreams, sounds like a win-win world, right?

Not necessarily so. In fact, many of us have found one big obstacle-- a mindset that dictates: "It's not okay to eat the foods we love." Furthermore, this "illogi-con" states: "Because you are overweight-- bland and boring food is your only option."

There is also a clause that proclaims: "You aren't the '*type*' who gets to have the life of your dreams."

Scores of us heard variations of that same diet dissertation. It seems that deprivation had become a way of life.

Is this mindset insurmountable? Absolutely not, but it does take screening the broadcasts from the "dictator of doom." Otherwise, we will continue on the same sad path, littered with guideposts of failure and gloom.

Is this dis-ease incurable? Definitely not! The antidote is more Self-love, Self-exploration and Self-indulgence.

In order to get into a winning mode, we need to practice some new principles, which I lovingly call "The Art of Self-Indulgence."

As with all art forms, it takes practice, focus and techniques to step our way to the farthest corners of fulfillment. So let's take the first step.

First Step: Defining our terms.

> ## Self: (capital "S")
>
> The part of a being (often called the higher self) that thinks and acts in a conscious, spiritual, and rational manner. This Self not only desires to create its own optimal life, but also strives to create the greatest good for everyone.
>
> ## self: (small "s")
>
> There is also a lower self, often called the subconscious. This is the part of the mind that, left unchecked, sabotages our lives. Most likely it started doing so during childhood.

The lower self draws illogical conclusions like: "My boss is a nasty, controlling wench, so I will eat a whole cheesecake. I'm the boss here!"

Or: "I want to be a dancer, doctor or designer but I'm not talented, smart or deserving... so I'll have a double-chocolate brownie with my triple cappuccino and get some sugar/caffeine satisfaction instead."

This lower self-defeater might mean well. It just doesn't want us to get too cocky or out of our league or to act like prima donnas. Does the phrase, "Who do you think you are?" ring a bell?

> **Indulgence:**
>
> The act of yielding to one's highest desires and dreams.

Because most dictionaries put a negative slant on this word, I had to create my own definition. This form of indulgence means granting ourselves permission to go after our most cherished dreams and reach our highest goals. It doesn't mean treating ourselves like spoiled children-- at least not more than once a week.

> **Art:**
>
> A principle used to take any subject to its highest level.

Does this sound like work or (at the very least) severe discipline? Work, no. (We are no longer helpless children being bossed around by that Corporal of Condemnation.)

A commitment? Yes. A commitment to put some new pleasure principles into place and practice them diligently. By "diligence" I mean not only enforcing "Self care" when we're happy and feeling confident. We must be most diligent in practicing "safe Self" when we feel sad, defeated and depressed.

Next Step: Reading the next chapter, learning some techniques of indulgence and trying on this "dream lifestyle" for size.

Pleasure Principles

Since we are launching a new life, we can bid fond adieu to a few old habits that are not welcome guests upon our pleasure craft, *S.S. Self-Indulgence.*

We can start by saying farewell to the days of diets, deprivation and any other plan we went on and fell off.

Falling off a diet is just subconscious rebellion. Since we were dieting to please others and not enjoying the experience, we harbored deep feelings of "selling ourselves out."

We would stick to the program until that ever ready "rebel self" appears with her "up-yours attitude" and instructs us to forget this-- "It isn't working, so eat whatever you want!!!"

Now, we can finally put that rebel in her place. We can eat the things we desire-- but this time we treat ourselves to low-carb versions, dished up to the tune of: *"Doing good, feeling good and looking good!"*

New Attitude

So the next step is launching a new attitude-- an attitude with latitude.

Think of this new life plan as a privilege, not a punishment. We no longer have to face a plate of eggs and meat for breakfast. Morning starters can feature a menu of waffles, shakes or coffee cake.

Lighten Up

And when it comes to lunch, we can forget the boring broccoli/chicken breast special. Now we can dine on delicate crepes or blintzes, topped with sour cream and berries.

Our dinner doesn't have to end with the taste of steak or swordfish lingering on our palate. We can climax with cookies, cakes or anything else that has us singing, "Amen."

So down with diet-- up with indulgence.

A New Weigh

Now it's time to rid yourself of a weighty issue-- throw away your scale. That simple act is one of the most freeing things I have ever indulged in. Gone are the days of scale obsession and scale depression. We want to lose fat, not numbers.

It is so much more pleasant using clothing as a guide for checking changes in the body. (Not stretch pants!) Usually, body changes start from the top down.

Slipping into a smaller size is much more satisfying than looking at numbers on a machine. "Size 14" sounds a lot smaller than "170 pounds."   This method also keeps pleasure as an ongoing process-- not just applauding our-selves when we **reach** our goals.

In the past, I wouldn't allow myself to enjoy life unless I had achieved "body beautiful." Even when I had whittled down to a size 10, I still had voices taunting familiar put-downs: "Not firm enough, not cute enough—not young enough."

So, exile that scale to a deserted spot in the attic, basement or garage. In place of its icy facade, hang a pic-ture of a happy-looking person and a sign that reads, "Life Is Fun."

When I visit my doctor, I avoid the scale by saying that

I am on a weight loss program that forbids being weighed. Not one nurse has ever argued with me and when the doctor sees that I have healthy blood pressure and cholesterol levels, he is satisfied.

Throwing away that scale will actually take a whole lot of weight off-- your mind.

Quiet as a Clam

The third gift requires less of you-- less talking that is.

I offer the freedom to rid yourself of an old obsession and not discuss this new food plan with anyone. *(The doctor is the exception to this rule.)*

Take up new topics of conversation-- anything but diet and food. Our friends are definitely sick of hearing us harp on those subjects. In fact, aren't you?

How about focusing on an exciting vacation you are planning next summer or maybe talking about that new art class that has you really pumped? People will start to see you in a new light. You will start to see yourself in a new light.

A policy of silence is especially important in the beginning stages of this plan because we are already vulnerable to our own voices telling us: "It won't work!" The last thing we need is anyone else chiming in and casting skepticism our way.

It's not that we are trying to keep this a guarded secret; it's just that well-meaning people (who aren't happy with their own bodies) might try to give us a hundred reasons why this plan is too good to be true. (Remember that old lie?)

Everyone is an expert on weight loss-- but let's face it,

even doctors can't agree on the right way to take off pounds.

Once you start to see your own body change, be prepared for a barrage of questions. People will see you slimming down and want to know your secret. At that point, you might tell them; then again, you might not.

If I know a person is open and has sincere interest, it is probably a good idea to direct them to this book. Secondhand information is often confusing.

If I feel a person is just asking out of idle curiosity, I love to give a tiny smile and say, "Just loving myself more."

Ready for more Self-love? The next chapter introduces an important traveling companion for our new journey on this *Sea of Self-Exploration.*

Journaling
(Dreams to Reality)

Ready to board the vessel heading for the "Land of NuYu?"

If you're used to over-packing, forget it. The only thing we're bringing (besides our cache of low-carb sweets) is a journal.

These bound pages will not only help shed light on unexplored territory of our lives but also serve as a guide for reaching our goals and dreams.

This journal can also be used as a life raft in case we find ourselves overboard in one of life's stormy seas.

Does this sound simplistic? Probably. Simplicity is **under-rated** in this high-tech world, filled with over-priced, over-inflated promises.

Is this feasable? Of course. There are no high-priced experts to consult, no Mecca to reach-- **it's just you getting in touch with your Self.**

So, if you have searched countless books, tried a dozen different practices and still not found the answers-- perhaps your search is over.

I have tried everything from psychology to psychics, and though I have experienced marvels and profound wisdom-- **nothing** has been as practical or rewarding as sitting down with a journal every day and seeing my thoughts on paper.

Thoughts are far easier to handle on

the written page than when they are rampaging uncontrollably through the mind. It also feels safer to explore the past on paper, where we are able to keep painful incidents in manage-able containment.

After a year of journaling, I discovered an early child-hood incident that (decades later) was still making every day a dreaded awakening. It was a constant mystery to me that regardless of how well my life was going-- my mornings always felt like an entry into gloom.

Then one morning (while I was writing about how rotten I was feeling) it dawned on me. *As a child, I was terrified to wake up to the shame of a bed wetting accident.*

Thank goodness, that problem is ancient history, but the feelings were being relived on a daily basis. A simple discov-ery? Not at all! Mornings are a daily occurrence and now mine dawn on a much brighter horizon.

Get ready to shake up a few volcanoes and unearth a few gems from your past. This requires no dynamite. All we need to do, is start a new morning practice.

The Practice

Although there are countless books on journaling, this mini-introduction may prove invaluable for chipping away the boulders blocking your "Road to Ideal."

A gift of 30 minutes a day is all that's required for this writing adventure of self-discovery. Surely your new Self is worth half an hour?

Morning is the best time to write, before the burdens of the day come crashing down around us. This time is most productive because the deepest thoughts are closer to the surface after a night of sleep. I have also found that the answers to problems seem to come first thing in the morning (or while I'm sleeping). If I don't write them down right away, I tend to forget them.

Whenever possible, you should strive to write three standard-sized pages. However, I have learned to not be too rigid about the number of minutes or the volume of writing. Many have fallen away from this priceless practice because they missed a morning or found time to write only two pages. If you absolutely can't write first thing in the morning, find another time slot for Self-discovery. The more effort you put into this practice, the more progress you will gain.

Easy? Not always. But, like a cell phone, once you get used to it, you can't imagine how you lived without it. For an invaluable guide on journaling, I highly recommend Julia Cameron's book *The Artist's Way.*

Not a Work of Art

This journal does not have to be a cloth-covered, embossed work of art. In fact, any standard-sized notebook will do. (So far, this practice costs only pennies and minutes a day.)

Journaling does not demand that you be artistic or clever. This form of writing is a stream-of-consciousness stampede running unbridled across your pages. Don't worry about spelling, periods, commas or making sense. No judgment. No censoring. No holding back. Let it all out. (Make sure that no one is reading your journal except you.)

Sometimes this book might feel like a dumping ground-- but this is one time when it's actually valuable to litter.

3-D Revelations

Developing the habit of writing in a journal delivers a triple threat to the thoughts that have kept us chained to failure, sadness and lives less-lived. We can "lay low" the enemy with my 3-D Technique: Dump, Deploy and Define.

Given time, this approach can offer a welcome retreat from the past. Ready for that sabbatical? Then it's time to say good-bye to "Lucy Lowerself" and pack her bags of derision, deprivation and depression.

Remember to bless her (after all, she is a part of you)... thank her (she's leaving)... and then buy her a one-way ticket to an iceberg in the Antarctic. Let her pester a few penguins for a while. They don't speak English, anyway!

First Step: Dump

Start with stream-of-consciousness writing. Let your thoughts run wild and record whatever comes up. Sometimes this turns out to be pages of negativity, fears or anger. Other times it might just be a grocery list. Don't judge, just write.

Record in detail anything that is bothering you: the memory of last night's nightmare, an unspoken tirade towards a mate or an overwhelming "must do" list. Whatever comes up is good. It's better to have it on paper than bulging inside the brain, where it can grow, fester and take over the day.

Many times, beautiful words of joy, wisdom or even a poem will flower on this garbage heap. That's one of the gifts from spontaneous writing.

Upon finishing this clearing, you will be able to face the

day feeling at least more organized and less overwhelmed. You might even find that you feel like you are walking on air. (As it turns out, some of that garbage is pretty heavy stuff.)

It took me months to reduce that trash heap, but when it started to dwindle, I was delighted with a shiny new perspective.

Sometimes our lives require an emergency writing session, so I recommend traveling with a purse-sized journal. If you are hit by an overwhelming blast of sadness or a relentless urge to stop at Penny's Pie Shop, whip out your notebook and describe in minutest detail what you are feeling and why. It might be a snide remark your friend made or it could have been prompted by driving past a school and remembering that you always wanted to be a teacher. Often the voice of doom sneaks through the borders of "safe self" and blasts away newfound confidence.

Stay on the feeling; nail it to the wall. Continue writing until you reach some composure or a conclusion. Maybe this one incident will catapult you into a new career or maybe even free your spirit enough to have a good laugh.

Do it now, there isn't a better time to free yourself.

Second Step: Deploy

In that heap of garbage are a few ticking bombs, waiting to blow your new dreams to smithereens. Be on the lookout for those blasts of derision-- underline the "lay-you-low" phrases and put a big "Gotcha!" or a huge **"X"** across them. The following tale is one of my reckonings with a missile of destruction:

"Out of a Tailspin"

As I as coming to the end of writing this book, I was feeling like I had finally gotten this self-indulgence thing under control. Not so!

Suddenly, things went into a tailspin. Old Lucy Lowerself went on a rampage. The exchange went something like this:

Self: "Wow, this book is almost done. When it's a big success, I'll go on Oprah, tell everyone about 'Low-Carb Sweets' and start a happiness epidemic."

That thought threw "her" into gear and she retorted: "How can you go on Oprah? You aren't slim or wise! You should be willowy like Gwyneth and as wise as Ms. Angelou. You better jumpstart your weight loss and go on the grapefruit diet. I believe the intelligence issue might be a lost cause..."

"Stop!" I shouted, catching that demon in mid-breath.

Then I sat myself down, grabbed my journal and put good deployment tactics into practice. This is what I wrote:

- Fact: I am not going on another diet. I have found an eating style that is fabulous and I am slowly and happily changing my body.

- Fact: If I really want to jumpstart this whole thing, I can have more fun. There are activities I enjoy and never find time for, like dancing, swimming and cross-country skiing. I also want to refinish my old chest and take up hiking with the Sierra Club.

- Fact: I am on top of you, Lucy. I'm smart enough to see through your tricks. Even if I were a size 6, I wouldn't be slim enough or worthy enough. So "buzz off" is the phrase of the day.

In a nutshell, I can do the things I love to do, feast on my favorite foods and most importantly, love myself-- willowy or not. I'm starting to get it.

Third Step: Define

We must create a clear picture of where we want to go before we can reach that destination. That's how we turn dreams into reality. From now on, our journals become our compass to help map out the paths to those dreams.

In the past, we didn't reach or maintain our goals because we were getting knocked off course by tidal waves of subconscious subterfuge. We can now handle the "flotsam and jetsam of the mind" by using our journals to put our new ideals into concrete forms and reinforcing those ideals with daily writing sessions.

The following techniques are effective and enjoyable ways of creating our fantasy lives and bodies:

★ **Word pictures** are the original form of creation, "In the beginning was the Word," proclaims the Bible.

This unlimited verbal wealth is the alphabetical pallette for creating your own personal dreamscape.

Use your journal to craft these sumptuous stories with you as the star, who always reaches her goals and highest aspirations.

Is your story set in a 3000 square foot log cabin... or an adobe charmer in the dessert...or perhaps, a glass mansion overlooking the Pacific?

This saga predictably begins with you coming into the scene looking like your custom-tailored vision of loveliness.

The light catches your flowing... bouncy... or perfectly coiffed hair? One immediately notices your petite, strong or lissome body; graced with irresistible breasts, (why not?) fabulous legs and a flat, firm tummy.

Of course, go crazy with your attire. Try silk, cashmere, heavy muslin or country denim. Get the picture?

Sometimes the results of these word pictures are astounding. It's like shooting off a rocket towards the future-- the clearer the image, the greater the possibility of reaching your "Planet Perfect."

★ **Affirmations** are powerful phrases describing your aspirations in the present tense; meaning you are already in possession of this ideal. For instance:

"I (name) love my healthy, slim energetic body."

"I (name) am slim, sexy and lovable."

"I (name) enjoy living in my slim, supple, strong temple."

"I (name) am attracted to foods and activities that create beauty and health."

Write each affirmation at least 10 times. Put your favorites on the refrigerator, tape them on the dashboard of your car and put them in your billfold.

Make up your own phrases to describe your goals and dreams. Any words that uplift you or make you smile.

You believed the old lies.
Why not believe the new truths?

★ **Visualizations** are an ideal method to set dreams in motion, especially for those who are more adept with pictures than words. I often cut out pictures from magazines depicting my ideal life and collage the cover of my dollar store journal. It's also fun to create a poster of an ideal scene. Hang it in a prominent place for inspiration.

I collaged my notebook with a picture of me in my perfect body, soaking in a Japanese tub in a wooded meadow. *The day after I made the collage, I saw an ad for a Japanese tub that was actually affordable-- proof positive that this visualization stuff works quickly.*

Sometimes I use an inside notebook cover as a section devoted to the lower self and her machinations. I usually find a picture that depicts her hideous image and then write every negative word or phrase that she has used to destroy my dreams. I finalize the procedure by putting a big black **"X"** through the whole scene. Putting a demon in that dimension diffuses its power.

I started drawing very simple pictures of my dream body as the third page of my journaling sessions. These pictures point out thin thighs, a flat tummy and always include a big glowing heart. After all, I don't want to lose sight of the most important principles:

> **"A queen-sized heart is far better...**
> **than a petite-sized body."**

I find that journaling opens a gateway to spiritual awareness. Once we quiet the noise of the wounded ego and flush out the demons of denial, we are closer to our higher Self, the Spirit. Whatever your spiritual beliefs may be, you will have a clearer channel to hear this *"voice of truth."*

For myself, I have discovered the God of love, generosity and endless support. Many times I have journaled about some overwhelming problem and have been amazed to have the answer show up on paper-- often in the same day. Sometimes it is not the answer I might have sought, but eventually I discovered that the solution was exactly what I needed. Most of the time, I am overwhelmed by the generosity of the Creator, for I have been blessed with more abundance than I could have ever imagined.

So keep writing, keep seeking and expect miracles.

Ashley's Journal
(A Window to Discovery)

Ashley is a pretty, vivacious brunette with a commanding presence. She appears to handle the world with authority but internally she battles with herself over weight issues. This has been an on going problem since high school.

The single woman enjoys loving relationships with friends and family, but finds it difficult to handle a long-term relationship with a man. She feels she can't really open up to guys because her love/hate relationship with foods is still a closet issue for her.

She confesses that every time she starts losing weight (on one diet or another) she eventually blows it when the sweet smell of cookies, candy or anything chocolate lures her into a web of temporary satisfaction. No matter how strong her resolve, she finds herself on a sweets binge that ends in a huge case of shame and remorse.

The 32-year-old advertising executive says that a low-carb lifestyle has worked best for her except for the absence of desserts and starchy comfort foods. Without this occasional indulgence, she feels doomed to failure.

A mutual friend turned her on to the principles of Low-Carb Sweets, which she confessed sounded too good to be true. Being a gourmet cook, she was eager to buy the book and give the recipes a try. She also agreed to apply the principles of the book and faithfully keep a journal in hopes of gaining some insight into her destructive eating patterns.

The following excerpts were created from

several months of her daily entries. I won't give away the ending.

So Far, So Good

I am excited to try this new low-carb sweets program. Can this possibly work for me? I have tried everything else and I love sweets, so I'll give it a try.

I bought enough supplies to last for a week, and although it set me back a little, I can cut back on the chicken breasts and other boring proteins I have grown so tired of.

Yesterday, I started with a big pecan waffle (drenched in butter and sprinkled with cinnamon and the "almost sugar" stuff.) I must admit it was fabulous and, at coffee break, I wasn't even tempted by the donuts. So far, so good.

I'm supposed to stop weighing myself, so I guess I'll put the scale in the closet. It is going to take some getting used to not going through that depressing morning ritual. Ha!

A Sweet Pact

I made a batch of "Fabulous Fudgies" and they are so good that I almost feel like I'm cheating.

I took some with me when I went to meet Jamie at Starbucks.

She sat there somberly in her "size 4" jeans as I explained that the cookies were actually low in carbohydrates and helping me lose weight.

"Yeah sure," she said in a stoic tone as she sipped her non-fat mocha latte. Only I know she will go home, down a pint of "Chunky Monkey," and then throw up because Bill didn't call.

I'M MAKING A PACT WITH MYSELF TO NOT TELL ANY-ONE ABOUT THIS LOW-CARB SWEETS PLAN!!!!!

I'll Do It My Way

Last night was a disaster at Mom and Rob's house. A celebration for Susan's engagement to Mark Copowitz. (Not my cup of tea, but very rich.)

Of course, as lusciously "lipo-ed" Susan showed off her two-carat diamond, she passed me her surgeon's card during dessert and whispered, "Try lipo! It's a sure ticket to marital bliss."

Luckily, I had some brownies waiting in the fridge at home, so I passed on dessert and the card. When I got home, I savored each morsel of that rich walnut brownie. I caught myself humming the tune, "I'll do it my way."

Office Politricks

My boss Zeke (the sneak) and I met with the vice president to discuss our new ad campaigns. Zeke took all the credit for the "Boxers in Boxers" ad (which I did from conception to corrections) and when the president asked why we were behind deadline on the Jamison campaign, he gravely said, "I'll talk to Ashley about that in private."

That big lying jerk! That was his project.

I was so furious; I went into the lunchroom and went straight to the machine to buy those cookies I love.

Then I remembered.

I had some low-carb Luscious Lemon cookies in my purse. So, I calmed down and tried to enjoy my cookies with a drink. I still secretly contemplated throwing Zeke down the elevator shaft.

Hooray! I made it through a disastrous workday. I wonder if this sweet thing is working?

Eating the Fridge

I'm feeling so depressed. Mom called in tears and told me that Nana Jean has stomach cancer... with little time left.

My Nana... always there for me... so sweet... my best family.

I feel like eating the fridge. I need something comforting. A cup of tea and cookies?

Seems like a shallow time to worry about food. But I might as well take care of myself. Glad I still have those cookies. Saved again.

I'm learning how to make it through the "hurts" without hurting myself.

I'm going to spend a lot of time with Nana, while I still have her.

Shake It Up

I should go to the gym today, but I just feel like staying home and wallowing in my sadness about Nana.

Besides, I'm starving and if I eat I'll be too full to do aerobics. Then again, if I don't eat, I'll feel too weak to work out.

I know, I'll have a high protein shake and a couple of those lemon cookies.

Shake and cookies, this isn't too bad.

Bad Hair Day

Tonight's my date with that guy I met at the gym. I was excited about getting my hair done; I wanted to look great.

My stylist, Anthony, decided to give me a new look. A new look all right-- I look like I came out of an Egyptian tomb.

He cut my bangs way too short. How could he forget my hair shrinks when it dries?

Why didn't I say something? For the prices he charges. I should look like a model.

I was so tempted to stop at 31 Flavors on the way home, but I remembered I had some brownies stashed in the freezer. Oh yeah, I noticed my new jeans are a little loose. I guess this is actually working. Amazing, I haven't felt deprived at all.

Next time I'm definitely saying something to Anthony.

A Cheer for Psyllium

Although this isn't a subject I want to broadcast, I am experiencing an amazing transformation. I have battled with constipation since I was a kid but, since I have been doing the low-carb sweet thing, I'm a transformed anal-retentive. It's amazing. Must be the psyllium in the waffles. Another great change is that my skin has cleared up. Hooray, I'm loving this.

Beautiful Heart

Put another big "D" on the calendar for disaster. I met with Aunt Jessica today for lunch.

I was feeling pretty cute and I can see that I am getting a little slimmer. I didn't say anything to her about losing weight and waited to see if she noticed.

Halfway into lunch she passed me a brioche and I said, "No thanks." She did it again, and again I said, "No thanks." Then she just looks me in the eyes, pats my hand and says, "Don't worry honey. We don't care if you are fat. We love you because you have a beautiful heart."

I felt like she kicked me in the stomach.

I got home and hit the cookie jar— and then started in on the cheesecake I had in the refrigerator.

I'm afraid to wake up tomorrow and see what damage I have wrought.

Amazing Morning

Amazing! I woke up this morning and I'm not feeling bloated, my face isn't puffy and I don't have that hungover feeling. I slipped on my jeans, and they are still loose.

When I actually sat down and totaled my carbs from last night's freak out, I only had about 37. One piece of regular chocolate cake has more than that.

Thank you— thank you— this is amazing. I can do this. Today, it's back to moderation.

I'm going to say something to Aunt Jessica when I'm slim and gorgeous. I think I'll tell her that I love her, even though she's wrinkled, because she has a nice big mouth— Ha Ha. Okay, I'll lighten up a little.

Chocolate Dilemma

I want to make chocolate chip cookies this week, but can I really be trusted with a bag of chocolate chips in the house?

I'll make that decision tomorrow when I shop for the week. Let's see, the chocolate chip cookies have only about 2 grams each... there is a lot of fiber. Hmm... I wonder?

Relaxed and Glowing

I did something I have always wanted to do. I went for a

massage and body wrap at Lumiscent.

I came home feeling relaxed and glowing. I can actually see that the skin on my thighs is less dimpled.

For a treat, I made the chocolate chip cookies-- yes, I bit the bullet and bought the chips. Like a real "star," I only ate three of my favorites while the chocolate was still melted.

I put the bag of chips in the freezer, and it's not even a temptation. I feel strong. I could give a Tarzan yell.

Homemade Happiness

I am so mad. Last night I was too tired to make any sweets (I forgot to plan ahead,) so I stopped at the store.

I had seen these great-looking bars that say "2½ carbs" on the front of the package.

After I had eaten the whole thing, I checked the label for the protein count. and I was so shocked to see that the bar actually had 27 grams of carbs. When I looked at the front again, it said (in small print) 2½ carbs of sugar. I feel ripped off.

I'm so glad that I can make my own stuff and actually know what I'm getting. Hooray for "Low-Carb Sweets!" Homemade happiness.

Feel Small, Get Big

Last night I promised myself that I was going to take Shaqs for a walk before dinner. I started watching something on the tube and before I knew it, it was dark outside. I felt really guilty and noticed I ate a bunch of cookies when I wasn't even hungry.

When I don't keep promises to myself, it makes me feel small. When I feel small, I want to make my body big. Weird, huh?

From now on, I only want to make promises I plan to keep. Wow, I think I've discovered a key to my heart.

A Lose-Lose Situation

I just realized that I don't really believe I am entitled to eat delicious food.

I feel like a loser-- who feels deprived if I don't eat things I love-- and guilty if I do.

Now that's a lose-lose situation. When did that all start?

Attention Makes Me Feel Vulnerable

This morning I noticed my stomach feels flat and my face looks really slim. This is throwing me into a panic. I have a huge urge to eat out-of-control.

Why am I afraid of being slender?

Maybe it's because I don't want all the attention that comes from being beautiful. It makes me feel vulnerable.

I want to go inside and hide in my wonderful secure fat cave. I am going to have to stay on "self-sabotage alert" all day. This journal is staying by my side.

"Self Sabotage Alert"

I am managing to stay on this low-carb eating program while I'm struggling with my fear of being thin. Who knew?

I'm afraid of becoming too successful because then people will attack me.

And what if I let my spiritual self down by becoming too narcissitic?

Do I really think I can have it all? Who do I think I am?

If I actually get slim, I will have to go after what I really want instead of just "futzing" around with this eating business.

Aha! Or, as Oprah would say, "A light bulb moment."

Person of My Dreams

I have managed to keep eating low-carbs and not freaking out at the thought of being my gorgeous Self. That sounds like insanity, even to me.

Speaking of dreams, I made the most unbelievable treat... the Chocolate Almond Clusters. They were delicious and it only took about 10 minutes to make them.

I took a few to work for coffee break. While I was eating them, two people came over and hung around my desk, waiting for me to offer them some. I didn't have enough, so I acted like I didn't notice. (Me first!) Tomorrow I will make a double batch and bring some to share.

Fat Cave

I brought the Almond Clusters to work and no one could believe I made them.

And they were really skeptical when I told them they were low-carb.

I gave in and told them about the "Low-Carb Sweets" book. Jan and Maddie were so impressed, they both ordered copies online. I should have charged a finder's fee.

Oh, I forgot, Eric, the cute guy in the art department, told me I have beautiful eyes. I noticed he was actually checking out my butt. I guess I am looking better.

I now have to make a special effort not to get frightened and jump into my "fat cave."

Home Sweets Home

I am feeling so stressed. I have until tomorrow to come up with new ideas for the McKinley ad campaign. Zeke agreed to let me work at home because there are too many interruptions at the office.

Right now I am feeling so anxious, that after every few paragraphs, I feel a compulsion to go to the cookie jar and scarf a few. I am definitely not hungry, but I keep running to the kitchen and returning with a cookie.

I guess I have always handled stress with food. My magic fix. Oh well, I probably had only 12 carbs in the six cookies I ate.

Maybe I'll try going outside and breathing some fresh air or have a jump on my new trampoline. There I go... a good solution.

Maybe just one more cookie.

A Few Days Off

I haven't written in my journal for days. It's been incredibly hectic at work, but I finally finished the presentation. We showed the proposal to McKinley and he loved the whole concept. (My baby.)

Everyone praised me-- especially the big boss. Zeke couldn't claim any of the campaign as his. I took advantage of this wonderful turn of events and asked for a few days off.

When they said yes, I could hardly contain myself. I wanted to dance on the desk. I am so glad to be back writing in my journal. I felt a little lost.

Prepared for Pleasure

I called Jamie last night because she works at home and can take time off. We decided to take a trip to Desert Hot Springs. I love the desert.

I will bring along a batch of cookies, a can of protein powder and a secret stash of fudge. I am not going to get caught unprepared.

We found a gorgeous hot spring spa online that was less expensive because it's off-season. The place looks divine!

Luxuriating

Since we have been at the spa, I feel like a queen. All I have on my schedule is soaking in the mineral springs, swimming in the pool and reading my favorite magazines while luxuriating in the sun.

First thing Jamie said when she saw me in my swimsuit was that I looked "a little" slimmer.

I thought she was being kind, but Jamie is not free with her compliments. I didn't bring up what she said about low-carb sweets, but I think she now sees that it is working.

I'm still not weighing myself. (I'm loving that part.)

Boutique Boogie

We went to one of those outrageously-expensive boutiques. Jamie loves those trendy little shops. (The kind where I never find anything in my size.)

I fell in love with a darling red dress. The salesperson asked if I wanted to try it on. I was shocked; usually they ignore me. At first I hesitated, but I gave in and took the dress into the dressing room. To my amazement-- the dress went over my hips and looked fabulous.

I hesitated about spending so much money but I decided to celebrate-- and besides, I deserve it.

I wore my blazing red beauty to dinner and two handsome men made a very big play for me... not ("size 4") Jamie... me.

I am feeling great. It's been only six months since I started this eating plan and all I can say is "Hooray for Low-Carb Sweets."

I'm a long way from being skinny, but I like myself more and I'm loving this Self-indulgence.

What's not to love?

"Blowing It"
(With Style)

When I first began thinking about writing this book, I went to a seminar for writers and publishers. I had a lot of trepidation about the project. Was there really a demand for such a subject?

At the start of the seminar, I made friends with a charming woman. She had a Ph.D. in education and wanted to publish a textbook on how to teach young children to be creative writers. (She had been teaching the subject for years.)

I felt a little hesitant when I said that I was writing a cookbook. But, when I told her the title, she looked at me, put her card in my hand and said, "Let me be your first customer."

She went on to tell me her story, a tale that is familiar to many of us.

Just the day before the seminar, her demanding schedule had her working overtime and she hadn't even taken time for lunch.

That night, on the way home, she stopped at a bakery outlet and bought a box of chocolate-covered donut holes. (A real bargain.)

Her rationale was: "I'll eat one to tide me over until I get home and make dinner. My family can eat the rest for dessert."

Well, 16 donuts later, she arrived home disgusted with herself and too full to eat dinner-- much less start cooking.

One Slip and It's an Avalanche

Like many of us, she confessed she felt out of control.

"I do eat low carbohydrate meals most of the time," she said, "but one slip and it's an avalanche."

During the break in the seminar, I shared some of my low-carb cookies with her. One taste and she said, "Get that book out!"

There are many of us looking for a way out of this food nightmare, often called "binging."

I don't really like that term because of the horrifying connections it brings to mind-- an isolated "closet" thing that no one does or talks about in public. I prefer to use the term "blowing it" because everyone blows it in one way or another. (It's almost considered a charming behavior.)

My beautiful friend Rosie had her unique form of blowing it-- big time.

This tall, slim social worker never kept food in her house. She always ate her meals in restaurants with friends. But she confessed to her own "secret ritual" for when life got too tough.

Rosie would graciously drive alone to five different restaurants and order pie and coffee. She would demurely sip and dine on each indulgence, then finally drive home with no one the wiser-- except her body, which was already suffering the effects of sugar sluggishness and her spirit which felt saddened and defeated.

Most of us are not that disciplined when we feel the urge to go out of control. When the craze kicks in, we want our "comfort" in the privacy of our own nests. The good news is that we can make our nests a safe haven and occasionally give ourselves permission to go overboard with low-carb sweets.

> *These sweets are a blessing at times like this. It's like riding the mechanical bull-- you experience the ride without getting the stuffing kicked out of you.*

This sweet satisfaction eliminates a "sugar stampede" on your body, brain and ego.

So, if life does come crashing down on you-- and you give in-- do it with a safer placebo. If you have to prepare something in a hurry, waffles work well, because you can eat a couple drenched in the topping of your choice and feel really full and satisfied.

One Bad Day Does Not a Lifetime Make

When it's all over, so what? Life gets tough and we are getting stronger every day. So forgive yourself for whatever-- admire your strength in starting a brand new day-- and get on with your wonderful life.

No matter what a rotten day you might have had or how badly you have blown it, there is one thing to remember: "One bad day does not a lifetime make."

People With Weight Issues Swallow Their Anger

In order to prevent future "blowing it" episodes, it is important to keep a close watch on emotions. People with weight issues tend to swallow their anger.

If we don't let this anger out, we will probably find ourselves packing in a whole lot of food to keep it down.

I am not suggesting we let our anger take us on a dangerous ride, but we should always use our **feelings** as a gauge to tell us what's important. If it weren't actually important to us, we wouldn't react so strongly, right?

Even little things need to be brought to light. If, during a conversation, you start to feel a twinge of discomfort, stop and look at it. I even stop the conversation in mid-sentence and say: "I am feeling uncomfortable about that remark." You don't have to say it in an angry way.

Sometimes the remark was not intended to harm, and other times it actually was a big zinger aimed straight towards the heart. Even if the person denies it, let **your feelings** be your guide. Why should we let other people's actions or words make us feel uncomfortable and cause us to go on a food rampage?

If it is absolutely inappropriate to say something, you can journal your way to absolution. Tell all-- write what you really want to say. Maybe you will discover a comfortable way to actually confront the situation.

The most important point is that **your feelings count**. Your own reality is the only reality you own. If something feels wrong, **trust yourself**.

24 Hour Makeover

A 24-hour makeover may sound like winning a day with a stylist of the stars, but actually it's a simple technique to turn any day into 24 hours of dazzle.

This whole concept started for me after watching Oprah Winfrey's "After the Show" program on the Oxygen Channel.

Oprah, a very wise and wealthy woman, confessed that she wished she could be her own best friend. She explained that she wouldn't think twice about spending $60 on a book for a friend, but actually balked when it came to spending it on herself.

It seems that self-denial is running rampant-- especially among women. I decided to sleuth my way to the top of this mountain of meagerness and garner unique solutions to combat this stingy monster.

So I put my head in the mouth of that "dragon of denial" and said, "Self, I'm on your side."

I made up my mind to give myself an entire day of self-approval and satisfaction.

I didn't have to go to a spa or take a vacation-- I just made up my mind to find pleasure and self-approval in everything I did for an entire day.

The whole day turned out to be an unexpected delight! Even the pile of mail on my desk turned into Mount Pleasure.

Unto Thine Own Self Be "Fru Fru"

I finished writing in my journa, then started clearing my desk so I could get to work on the book.

The Victoria's Secret catalogue caught my attention. Usually I just peruse a few pages and wish I could either afford some lovely thing or, at the very least, fit into their size range.

Today, I decided to check it out with a new attitude. I made up my mind that if I found something really fabulous, I would order it.

It was love at first sight when I came upon a pair of great wool/spandex pants. I needed a new pair and these were perfect. I checked the sizes. My size? Dare I? Yes!

I ordered the indulgent apparel (even though they were twice what I usually pay for pants) and it felt fabulous. I even ordered a gorgeous orchid wool sweater to make the outfit complete.

That act prompted me to clear out my closet full of bargain clothes that I don't even like. And while I'm at it, I'll discard that pile of boring black clothes, too. So, I am making myself a promise that from now on I am only buying things that sing to me.

I am looking at the item first-- instead of the price tag. A new manifesto: ***Unto thine own self be "fru fru."***

Gifts of Hope

The World Vision catalog, "Gifts of Hope," was in the pile of mail. It's a book of life-improving gifts you can buy for needy people around the world. As I looked through the book, I became totally sold on this novel concept of gift-giving. Since my husband and I don't really *need* anything for

Christmas, I made up my mind to buy a goat for an African family. One goat not only provides a family with milk, cheese, butter and yogurt but also can be a source of income.

This is true self-indulgence. I gave myself a happy heart.

A Bright Reminder

With the pile of mail put away, I sat down to write. I eyed a lovely lavender-scented candle that has been on the shelf for weeks. I had been waiting for a party or some special occasion to burn this beauty. I decided to throw *myself* a party and lit up my life with this simple act of opulence. My soul sang, "Yes."

Anger Alert

I received a phone call from someone who (frequently and in a very sneaky way) makes me out to be wrong. Usually I let the zingers pass me by but today, since I was feeling so self-indulgent, I decided to speak up. "Hey, wait a minute... I want to go back to something you just said...."

It felt wonderful. I made a vow to stop swallowing my anger and denying my reality. This self-indulgence stuff was becoming life changing, and I hadn't even left my desk.

I felt a new power.

A Walk on the Sensual Side

Since today is a new adventure, I decided to try a different path for my morning walk with Sheba, our German shepherd.

It was exciting exploration, climbing unfamiliar steep

hills and scouting new terrain. I was stopped by a strange cactus, tall like a tree but bumpy like a brain cactus. This eye-catcher made me pause and ponder the myriad of marvels I probably pass by every day because I "just don't take the time to see.

As we approached a charming little cottage, I was arrested by a fragrance I have loved since I lived in the mountains of Oregon... the powerful, intoxicating scent of wild roses.

Obviously, I *see* beautiful roses all the time, but this rose bush was a real "stop you dead in your tracks fountain of fragrance." I took huge breaths of the exotic sweet smell and walked on. Indulgence? I would say so.

Cookie Muncher

When I got home from my walk, I was hungry but did not feel like bothering with a big meal. I was only craving cookies.

It took me 15 minutes to whip up a batch of Fabulous Fudgies, which I happily munched while watching my favorite decorating show. That 30-minute break made me feel indulged and ready to get back to work on the book.

I feel fabulous, and still half the day to go!

I created this poem:

Tee hee
Tee hee
It feels good
To be me!

Sunset Serenity

My Self-serenity was spilling into evening, as I drove to the store to pick up a few groceries. I was captured by the setting sun, splashing the horizon with brilliant strokes of pinks and purples. I rode with the windows down, inhaling the fresh, chilly air. Breath, precious breath.

When I arrived at the store, I noticed an obviously down-and–out young man sitting on a bench near the shopping carts. Usually I just reach in my purse for a buck, but this time, I said, "Good evening, how's it going?" When he looked up, I stared directly into his eyes and reflected my own warm feelings towards him.

The flash of light in his eyes startled me. I felt a bittersweet tenderness seep into my heart, as we casually commented on the beautiful sunset.

I asked if I could pick him up anything while I was in the store.

He hesitated, and then admitted he was hungry. On the way back to my car, I brought him a deli sandwich and a drink. He helped me unload the cart and flashed me a warm smile as I drove off.

I arrived home feeling happy-hearted and humming the Beatles lyrics, "I get by with a little help from my friends."

What a way to end the day.

This Self-indulgence might be impossible to contain!

Dreams are real...

and life is a dream.

Stephen Sweeney

Index